Fred Marshall, aged about twenty years old

First Published in 2008 by the editor
JOHN MARSHALL
12, Morningside
Dawlish, Devon
EX7 9SL

Telephone: 01626 888798

Thanks and Acknowledgements:

I am indebted to the following:

1) for permission to use photographs of Sleaford Union Workhouse
Dr. Simon Pawley of Sleaford
Peter Higginbotham www.workhouses.org.uk

2) for advice and help from
Wendy Walder of Sleaford Library

3) for advice from
Muriel Bradshaw of Dawlish

4) for their help and courtesy
Swiftprint of Dawlish

5) for help with my computer/printer literacy
Polly Marshall and Tim Dudding

6) for her forbearance during my work on this book
Jill Dudding my partner

Thanks .... John Marshall.

Chapters:

Best Wishes
John Marshall
12th March 2008

Major Themes In The Book:

Beliefs

Childhood Pranks

Church And Chapel

Clothes/Furniture

Entertainment

Farm Work

Food And Drink

Health

Schools

Trades

Transport

Welfare/Politics

Wild Life/Pets/Love Of Countryside

Workhouse Life

Reference to place names mentioned in text

NOTE: The content centres on the three villages: Buslingthorpe/Faldingworth, Newton Toft (Market Rasen) and Waddington/Harmston.

Chapter 1
"Let the Little Bugger die!"

"Let the little bugger die!" was the advice given to my mother by a fellow inmate at Sleaford Workhouse when I was born.

But I did not! Arrogantly, I like to think that, even at so tender an age, strength of character and bloody-mindedness allowed me to spite her and the world.

Sleaford Workhouse Being Demolished

My Mother, Victoria Jubilee Marshall, named after the 1887 event, was born out of wedlock to an Elizabeth Marshall and an Italian father who had connections with the Italian Embassy, and was fostered out when a month old. At the age of seventeen, following the death of her foster parent, Victoria was thrown on to the mercy of a very uncaring country and was forced into domestic service in a part of rural Lincolnshire, where for years she lived a very hard life.

When she was twenty one she became pregnant, supposedly by a rather wild farm wagoner, but plenty of rumours around had it that my father was a city dweller or the son at the Big House. As was the cruel practice in 'the good old days', women about to give birth to a bastard were sent either to the local asylum or the workhouse.

Victoria Jubilee's fate was to be sent to the Town Workhouse in Sleaford and that's where I came in. I was just another BASTARD BRAT born on March 31st 1909.

Victoria Jubilee Marshall, Fred's mother at about 50

My mother and I had to stay there for over a year, during which time I was christened Frederick William Marshall. The old ladies resident there, I later learnt from my mother, 'completely spoilt me'. What being spoilt meant in such a degrading place, was only to be revealed to me on my second "imprisonment" in a similar establishment in Caistor in a few years time.

The local Guardians at Sleaford tried to 'persuade' my mother to leave me in the Workhouse when she decided to leave, but she brought me out and obtained dingy lodgings in the city of Lincoln working as slave labour in a factory.

I was left helpless as a baby and later as a toddler with a large family in our new 'home'. The other children used to pinch and scratch me and I was shut in a large cupboard when I cried for any reason.

So, when "the little bugger" did not die, mother was determined to get me out of the hell-hole and eventually found a position as housekeeper to a widower, Tom Lilley, who lived in a cottage at Moorby near Horncastle. He had three grown up children. Tom and my mother were married within three months and at last I had a real father. Over the years, in his simple, rural way he proved to be a wonderful dad.

Life in the country in the early part of this century, was still 'feudal' and everyone knew their place despite all the efforts of the reforming Lloyd George's Liberal Government. Those at The Big House still ruled and my stepfather had to work seven days a week as a garthman or stockman milking cows, for very low agricultural wages and a tied cottage. His life and family were all but controlled by the squire.

Tom was a rather religious man, attended the chapel regularly, never drank or smoked and thought the theatre an evil. However, had he approved of such 'pleasures' he could not have afforded to indulge in them.

At this time we lived in an old farm cottage. You could pick cherries off a tree growing up the front of the house and old fashioned roses climbed up the wall. There was a tempting orchard to play in and the apple trees hung partly over a tinkling stream. I remember a large field of buttercups, bobbing cowslips and the kingcups in the marshy areas.

We had poultry to look after and it was my job to collect the eggs. Sometimes I would throw eggs at the barn wall and watch the hens eat them, the cannibals! There was an old hen we called Thiefy because she used to steal from the kitchen. Once we had visitors and Thiefy provided the dinner. It saddened me, but I learnt quickly that such was part of the country law. At the age of five or six rural life had its attractions and in spite of the harsh working life of my mother and stepfather, for me it seemed almost idyllic and laid the foundation for my love of wild flowers and simple country pursuits which was to continue throughout my life.

My schooling had begun at Roughton which meant a long walk each way although there were no traffic dangers or undesirables to worry about.

World war one had begun but, without modern media, we heard

little about it. I remember my mother telling me, that, if I saw a man with a gun, I was to run home. Wounded British soldiers, discharged from hospital, helped on the farm to 'recuperate', before returning to the battlefields. We did see several hundred soldiers marching by on their way to the embarkation port. On another occasion platoons of soldiers rode by on bicycles accompanied by Officers on motor cycles. Rank and class privileges rankled even as a young child; I thought how unfair it was.

We recognised the German and Italian prisoners of war by the coloured patches on their uniform and would meet them when they worked cleaning out the pigsties and cowsheds. It was the time of the Spanish Flu epidemic and many of them perished in the great leveller.

At Christmas the choir and us children sang carols for the prisoners in the warehouse where they were billeted. The 'Krouts and Itis' clapped and clapped. The guards announced that they would not sleep that night. These men really were like any other mortals who appreciated kindness, but longed for home and family. Later this experience helped to confirm my growing belief in the futility of the war for whatever reason.

Part of Fred's original handwritten copy

Chapter 2
"Bargains and Retributions"

My stepfather stayed only a year or two on any farm, He was known as a confined worker. This meant that a farmworker was employed for a year and the boss then issued a 'bargain' so that he stayed on. The 'bargain', as it was ineptly called, ensured that the poor worker received a thirty stone pig a year, fire hundred weights of potatoes and a can of milk a day. On Good Friday you were loaned a horse and cart to go to the woods and collect a load of firewood.

All these so-called perks were completely offset by the fact that the wage was greatly reduced, so the family was worse off. This and similar practices, which had lingered on since Victorian Times but later became unacceptable after strong Trade Union pressure, seem in my old age to be hankered after by right-wing politicians. Does History repeat itself?

'Moving Day" for farm labourers was always April 6th. when 'contracts' expired. For the adults it was an emotional time but we children used to look forward to being loaded up with the furniture and setting off on the horse and dray for the new home and school. Motor transport was still a luxury.

One week after my seventh birthday we moved to Stainfield near Wragby. This village had a church with no churchyard and hung on one wall was a metal helmet. Gloves and rags which, I was told, had been part of a past warrior's battle dress, dangled from the ceiling. I sometimes visited the nearby church at Old Apley which only seated forty.

The Great War raged on and it was at about this time that I had begun to notice a few of its effects. German Zeppelins started to fly over on moonlight nights and I used to tremble and fear what consequences would befall us.

One day there was great excitement in the village. An aeroplane had crashed landed during a thunder storm. Fortunately the pilot had not been hurt. I had never seen a plane on the ground. This was a major event in my education. The propeller was damaged and eventually a new one was fitted. In the school playground we talked of nothing else and in our game shouted "contact" or "Petrol off" for weeks after. Some two years later near another of my village schools, a second aircraft came down in a field at lunchtime.

About ten of us set off to see this event. We stayed over an hour and on our return to school, the Headmaster lined us up to cane us on both hands. I thought I was being clever in growing confident mood and newly-acquired rebelliousness and told him as the leader, that we had not heard the bell. For my arrogance I got a double caning. This I resented, but in the best modern teaching practice, he later encouraged us to do an aircraft project.

A young Fred with two unknown ladies

An incident which I recall with some rancour, because I thought it was unjust, happened whilst at Stainfield School. There were two old maids teaching the younger children, a common practice then. One day they asked us for our opinions on the lesson we most disliked. When it was my turn, I announced honestly that I hated Scripture. At which point they called for three boos from the class. I thought how stupid it was to ask for an opinion and then humiliate me for expressing one they did not like. Perhaps the Lord was trying to get his own back for my 'blasphemy' when, a couple of weeks later on Christmas morning, I was pushing my present (a lovely toy yellow wheelbarrow) across the frozen pond when the ice gave way, I scrambled out safely but was it retribution?

Chapter 3
"Firing and Beating"

It was at Glentham, after another move, that I committed a stupid act. I had been gathering firewood - a task which usually fell to me - and it had begun to get dark. Although I would not admit it, I was petrified of the blackness of the country nights and secretly fetched a lighted candle so that the coal hole would seem less daunting. It still seemed eerie in there, even though we were used to such dim light. So without a thought for the consequences, I found some old rags and set them alight with my candle. Feeling less frightened I moved the wood into the coal house with the coal and left, believing I had completed my task successfully.

It was only in the early hours of the morning, as the building was some way from the house, that a neighbour smelt burning. By this time only a smouldering mass remained and what was left was dowsed with buckets of water from the pump. Four hundred-weight bags of charred potatoes stored in the coal shed, should have been an essential part of the family diet for months to come. Needless to say a good hiding from my hard-pressed stepfather was indicated. Mother said "You give him one!" But when Tom attempted to follow her initial advice she immediately retracted her statement shouting with equal fervour, "Don't you dare touch him." So, as usual, I went scot-free. I suppose that, because he was not my natural father, she felt the need to protect me.

I should point out that, during the war years, there was a shortage of matches. Therefore the farm men used first to make a mixture of saltpetre and water, find a broken file and sharp flint, dip rags in and let them dry. Next they hit the file against the stone holding the soaked rags next to it. The compound then began to smoulder, and finally the men lit their fags or pipe. I had seen them do all this many times whilst out in the fields, so perhaps I assumed that lighting old rags was a normal activity. Children have always imitated their elders, but I am not trying to excuse my 'crime'. No doubt, children nowadays who do senseless things, simply copy adults. Many of the scrapes we got up to went unrecorded.

During school holidays I would often have to 'tent' cows, letting them graze on the country lanes. I frequently milked them. There were few cars then in that area, not much traffic. Imagine allowing cattle to wander on the roads now! In very hot weather the beast were tormented by flies and would suddenly take off at a great pace. Often I was forced to run a mile or more to catch up with them and then had the job of persuading the animals, which had minds of their own, to go back home. This was no easy task for a young lad on his own. I got a shilling a day for the work. I also became very hungry and usually had eaten my dinner by ten o' clock in the morning. Therefore my next plan was to seek out a field of turnips or swede and supplement my meagre diet that way. Actually they tasted pretty good.

Being alone for so much of the day my imagination used to run riot. I was terrified of gypsies, tramps and any drunks, a fear doubtless inspired by the lurid tales told, whether true or imagined, by the older men. People have always been prejudiced against gypsies and still are.

Sometimes my mother and I used to work together on the farm picking potatoes at busy times and like many other children was off school on those days. I think the headmasters accepted it as normal country practice, so truancy was quite common in those days too.

In the Autumn we used to go with the guns at the local shoots mostly for beating. Fighting your way through the scrub and thorn hedges, having trekked through wet turnip and swede fields, produces severe scratches on the legs. It made them so sore. I could have cried, being only eight at the time. My mother never complained as she desperately needed the money. A job I particularly enjoyed was carrying the pheasants, rabbits and hares. Everyone received the princely sum of one shilling and piece of pork pie for dinner, which tasted very good. The ethics of shooting creatures for sport did not really concern me in those days, but as an animal lover I often think about it now. I am quite a sentimental person, but those who oppose country pursuits and field sports so strongly now, do not understand how wild life and farming are so dependent upon each other. I hate the cruel aspects of hunting and shooting but cannot see any alternative. Shooting is one of those country pursuits which has not greatly changed throughout my life, except that it is now big business. Those who practice it, often pay a high price for the privilege.

Walking was the only way of getting about, since public transport did not exist and we could not afford it anyway. We had only one pair of boots and so the soles wore out frequently. To have them mended, we had to walk from Glentham to a place called Tibbs Inn three miles away, take them off and wait whilst they were repaired. Perhaps a 'Shoes Repaired While You Wait" service sounds modern, but it was a day's outing.

The cobbler was a dear old man, who had a huge stove where we used to warm our feet on winter days. As he worked, he would tell us fascinating stories and could hold the interest of a couple of rough, country lads with ease. He would give us a hot drink and a piece of cake. Would his modern counterpart do that? We were intrigued that he climbed up the ladder from his work-room to his bed.

The nearest town, Market Rasen, was about six miles away and the nearest railway station five. We often walked there too.

When we needed a hair cut, a man would come to the house. He 'shaved' it short to last - a bit like a modern crew cut. He finished off by putting a basin over our head and trimming around it.

The cottage we lived in then was semi-detached and thatched. It was extremely damp and masses of beetles would invade the walls and old beams at night. I suppose it was normal then, but now I expect the pest control officer would be called in.

An orchard, which we used as a garden, belonged to our farmer landlord. That Autumn my mother was picking fallen apples, when the farmer arrived calling her a thief. She could be very direct and quick-tempered and told him: "to stick the apples up your arse!" We soon left that place and I cannot believe that the incident was not connected in some way.

Just before we were moved on, I was told by a group of lads at Sunday School, that the war was to end the next day. They proved to be right. That night a crowd of us headed into the village, banging buckets and kettles as we went. A farmer let us set up a bonfire in a field. It was our celebration, but the incident that cause most fun, was the sight of a rabbit emerging from the blaze with its tail on fire. I do not know whether the poor thing died, but I have thought of it with remorse many times. On the way home we woke the farmer up by singing 'For he's a jolly good fellow', but I don't know if he really was.

Chapter 4
"Smoking, Scrumping and Nesting"

Our next move was to Burgh-on Bain which had connections with Tennyson and 'Half a Hundred Bridges'. We lived in what was once a large pub, converted into four farm workers' dwellings. It was sited at a cross-roads.

The Peace Celebrations which followed soon after our arrival in the village were a great event in our lives. It was a time for the gentry to dispense charity and the local Lord of the Manor, Major Fox, provided the 'big do' at Girsby Hall. Over two hundred villagers tucked into traditional country fare including rabbit pie. A Tug-of-War competition was held in the grounds. At the end of the day his Lordship asked everyone if they were happy. I piped up: "One young lad hasn't had his sweets!" This was remedied directly and as a nine year old I felt justice had been done. Lady Fox signed and presented Prayer Books to all the children.

It was at this time that I joined the chapel choir. We lads would leave practice before the adults so that we could raid the Junior Master's orchard. On the way home, whilst eating our scrumped apples, we had heated arguments about sex and how babies where born. Some said it was through the breast, others said the belly button but we really had little idea about such matters. We just thought we did. We were all sure we knew what our parents got up to!

We attended school in Hainton, the next parish, and during the holidays we had great fun, climbing trees and jumping becks. One of my great joys then was to visit the dry quarries. We would take candles, light them and stand them in rabbit holes. We just sat there and talked. I have often thought about this lighted candle ritual in latter years, but still cannot understand its significance.

Our first efforts at smoking took place in the quarry, without, we reasoned, the fear of being discovered by disapproving parents. First we improvised with rolled brown paper which we 'smoked' until we spluttered and choked and our eyes ran. Then we graduated to 'hemlock' pipes. which had a simular effect. Our most treasured find was a discarded cigarette packet. We would sniff and sniff. Perhaps we were the forerunners of today's child sniffers, but although the experimentations were the same, the consequences were not potentially lethal.

The final 'triumph' in our smoking exploits came one day in the harvest field. The men had left their coats hanging on the hedge whilst they worked, so, not really thinking about the moral or practical results, I stole a packet of cheap fags from one of their pockets. As always, I wanted to impress my fellow gang members with my daring leadership. We all thought we were big men when we attempted to smoke them even though I now admit to being violently sick afterwards. The moment of glory, however, was short lived. One worker blamed another for the 'loss' and eventually the truth was uncovered. The man who had been falsely accused gave me a good hiding and I deserved it. Nowadays he would have been in serious trouble for assault, but he was right to do it. This episode ended our smoking escapades, at least for a time.

Earlier in the year we used to do a lot of bird nesting, particularly moorhens and magpies. The eggs were delicious when fried. Overgrown hawthorn hedges were common and contained numerous magpie nests. Nearly every pasture field had its pond, a fast disappearing feature at this end of the century, and it was there the moorhens constructed their nests, so we devised an alternative plan to plunder the tempting delicacies.

The strategy was first to pinch one of stepfather's beansticks and one of mother's precious table spoons, and second to tie the spoon to the stick. We plunged into the pond as far as we dared, stretched out the tool we had made balancing it precariously and attempted to scoop out the poor moorhen's prospective offspring. Sometimes we were successful and with practice improved our technique. Finally we painstakingly withdrew the quarry hand-over-hand and put the eggs in our pockets. With experience we found that if we left one egg in the nest for quite a time the confused bird would keep on laying until it finally forsook the nest.

We revelled in the activity then but we rarely remembered to return the spoon, and my mother often questioned their disappearance.

Chapter 5
"Killing, Boring and Tubbing"

The 'Pig-Killing' was a most important event in the household calendar. This took place about three weeks before Christmas. The unfortunate animal would be brought, without ceremony, out of its sty with a rope fastened to its head. It would be dragged upright and tied to the top hinge of a stable door. The local butcher was called in for his ritual slaughter. As he wielded the knife to slit the pig's throat, the squawling and screeching could be heard throughout the neighbourhood. To me, as a young lad used to the harsh ways of the countryside, the sound was truly terrible. When the blood had stopped flowing and the creature appeared to have breathed its last, it was hauled into a large, flat salting tub which was then filled with boiling water. All the rough hair was scraped off. The carcass hung for one day on a special scaffold. I used to imagine in a macabre way that it was a man!

When the 'body' had been cut down, it was divided into sides of bacon, hams and chines with the backbone. The head and feet were removed to make brawn. Some meat had to be set aside for pork pies and sausages. The lights and liver were made into haslet and sweetbreads. The offal was prepared on special dishes and as a long standing tradition given to neighbours. This was known as 'The Pig's Tray'. The intestines were thoroughly cleaned and washed for use as sausage skins, the bowel became tripe and the bladder served as a container for the lard - hence the expression 'a bladder of lard'.

After a day or two the salting tub, which was about eight feet long and eight inches deep, was brought into the pantry. The hams and sides of bacon were rubbed with salt and saltpetre where they remained for a month. Finally the meat was hung from hooks in the ceiling and used throughout the year. Nothing in this grizzly process was wasted. Those who visit the supermarket now to purchase their lean and plasticised pork products, neither know nor want to, anything about the animal's demise. I have to say that I hated fat cold bacon for the weekday breakfast, the very thought of it made me feel sick, but Sundays it was fried and I loved to dip my bread in the hot bacon dip. Sunday was also the day when my mother produced the preventative medicine of the era, namely a large spoonful of brimstone and treacle from a treasured stone jar in the larder. My recollections are not clear as to whether this concoction produced more nausea than the fat bacon, nor what ailments the mixture staved off.

At this time my stepfather was injured by a cow and sustained a double rupture. The only way to gain admission to the hospital was to obtain a card, known as a 'recommend', from the Vicar or the Squire. Needless to say it was not forthcoming and he had to wear a truss. There was no National Health Service and one wonders if certain politicians have their way, whether a return to the 'good old days' might see similar patronage or lack of it.

Tom found it increasingly difficult to carry out the hard farm labour seven days a week with his disability, and consequently had to see casual work. Thus the next spring we moved yet again to Buslingthorpe near Faldingworth.

The new boss lived in a moated farmhouse. He was a go-ahead person and had obviously seen the advantages of acquiring tractors and hay lifters. He employed contractors to bore for water. They stayed for about a year and found water at about twenty five feet, but continued to a depth of four hundred. In the school holidays I was thrilled to be allowed to start a small oil powered engine which washed the various tools.

Two young Canadians visited the farm on holiday. They found an old salting tub, placed a plank on it as a seat and launched it on the moat. Using a shovel as a paddle, they rowed around the farmhouse. I had watched their enjoyment with envy and next day noting that the coast was clear, decided to paddle single-handed around the course. The moat was overhung by trees and about ten feet deep at the time. Danger has always concerned the youth less than those of more nature years and I set forth in my Kon Tiki without a thought for my welfare. Having successfully negotiated the waters round the front of the house, in my eagerness to imitate the Canadians, I lost concentration and moved too far to one side of the tub.

The shallow craft began to take in water fast and I was left desperately clinging to the tub in the muddy water. Luckily the farmer's wife had seen my predicament from the window and rushed to help. I could not swim and have never learnt, so it must have been self preservation which forced me to push the tub to the edge of the moat. The farmer's wife was too terrified to be angry, but told me years afterwards that she was sure I would drown.

On one occasion we were rewarded with a rare sight. Three large 'charabangs' full of lucky trippers drove by on their way to the coast. Skegness or Mablethorpe, the likely destinations, might have been as far away as the south of France as far as 'us lads' were concerned, rather than thirty or forty miles.

Son John, Granddaughter Polly with Mascot the Dartmoor

A great pleasure for me was a visit to the Blacksmith's Shop on the villages where we lived. Horses were still used as the commonest form of transport on the roads and farms in their part of rural England just after the First World War, and nearly every village had its blacksmith. The unique, tangy smell of the smouldering hoof when the red hot shoe was nailed in place always stayed with me. Blowing the bellows was a great treat and all the trappings of the farrier, which were carefully maintained, fascinated me, as well as the skills he used when shoeing. He never needed to measure the horse's foot to choose the size or type of shoe, but knew each animal as an individual. My young granddaughter is a keen horse rider nearly seventy years on and it is interesting that the blacksmith's tools and methods have changed little. Modern technology seems only to have affected the power for the forge and provided the transport for the blacksmiths to travel to customers.

Another love then was the local Hunt Meet. Whatever merit there was in the arguments against hunting, the sight of the splendidly turned-out horses and their riders and the pack of hounds waiting for the Master to set off, was most impressive, and part of country life. We enjoyed following the Hunt on foot but always hoped poor Reynard got away. If we were asked which way the quarry had gone, we always sent the members off in the opposite direction from where we had last seen it. The gentry used to talk down to us. We hated it, but they never realised what we thought of their patronising ways. They still thought of us as a different breed of human being, rather like some misguided people do now about black people.

We played the usual games of the time: whip and top for the boys in Spring was a favourite, and shuttlecock and battledore for the girls - a forerunner of badminton I suppose. The girls also did a lot of skipping to various rhymes, some far from what you would expect from 'innocent' country lasses!

Often there was a spate of apple pinching, but if we had a penny or two we would visit the local farms, asking the owners to sell us some. Often they did not take our money and provided the apples, so the bosses could be good-natured.

Every Friday a man came from town with a horse and dray bearing fish and fruit. We used to find him during school dinner hour and keeping behind the dray would help ourselves to apples, oranges or whatever happened to 'fall off'.

The Co-op baker also arrived on Friday - a good day for us. We would contrive to meet him and open the gates, as we lived a mile along a cart track from the tarmac road. My mother used to buy four pound loaves each week and the bits on the side of the tin which had spilled over when baking, were so very good when new. If he had tea cakes left over, the baker would sometimes give us lads a few. I used to eat a lot of the bread and lard in those days - just think of the cholesterol. Another favourite was mashed swede sandwich.

Every morning I had to fetch the milk in the billy can before school, which meant walking two to three miles along rutted cart tracks. The milk was not treated in any way but we did not seem to be harmed by it. Health regulations would totally prevent that now, but its ironic that the modern child is probably less healthy because he does no walking, not even to school, being carried by car because of the traffic dangers to pedestrians on country roads.

We did not keep chickens at every place where we lived and then eggs were a rare food, which may surprise many who assume that such basic foods were always available to country folk of all classes. Telling the farmer's wife that it was my birthday she asked if I would like an egg or a penny. Well, I knew that eggs were then $1\frac{1}{2}$ d each, so, being a budding financier, I chose the egg. It was a good birthday present.

Chapter 6
"Reciting, Kissing and Reading"

At this time at Buslingthorpe we were 'Chapel', as people used to call it. This simply meant that we attended the Wesleyan Chapel even though we were C. Of E. I regularly attended Sunday School. In those days no one even thought of doing otherwise. It was a way of life.

My mother was blessed with an amazing singing voice. She performed current favourites in chapel, where she was lead singer and soloist and at village concerts. Much to my pride she was recorded on Edison Bell Records singing "The Holy City" and "Killarney", but I only discovered this much later and sadly have never been able to trace a copy. I assume she must have been noticed by someone influential even in our closed little world.

Tom Lilley with Victoria Jubilee

Every year there were celebrations and a special service known as 'The Anniversary'. All the children had to prepare 'Recitations' for the service and a cantata was performed. The recitation ordeal was terrifying and I quaked as it came to my turn. Not any more the bold, arrogant lad practising his piece at home in front of admiring parents or shouting that I could see an airship and was the first to spot it. Was this timid, mumbling little boy me? Yes. In the chapel I truly thanked God when it was over, and could then revert to the confident child I pretended to be.

The Monday of the Anniversary was a great day, not only because the ordeal was over but because of the activities which followed. We would all assemble outside the Chapel and there stood the decorated wagons and immaculately groomed farm horses, proudly displaying their coloured ribbons and sparkling harness. The farmers and labourers had been up since the crack of dawn preparing their pride and joy. A small organ or harmonium had been carefully man-handled on to the first wagon and lads vied with each other for the chance to pump the bellows. The organist, accompanied by the choir and 'us children' housed on the following drays, performed hymns and religious songs. As we travelled through the surrounding villages, stops were made at various points en route.

The day ended with a special Anniversary Tea with cold ham, cakes, jelly and tea. This annual feast was followed by races. There was always a scramble for sweets when large quantities were thrown on the grass. Often the young or timid children did not get any and I always thought it unfair. I have never believed in the survival of the fittest theory for humans. If man is civilised he should help the weak.

In the evening the grown-ups played a game called 'Kiss in the Ring'. A circle was formed and a couple danced into the ring. Everyone sang ' Here we come gathering 'Nuts in May'" - which should really should have been 'Knots of May' - "I am waiting for a partner. Now you're married you must obey. Chop the wood and muck the hay." They kissed and a second pair entered the circle.

This probably seems very innocent now and very sexist, but it was quite daring then. The 'marriage' in the game was certainly quick. Sexual relationships outside the marriage were publicly considered taboo and those born out of wedlock, as I was, were still stigmatised. However, people were no more 'moral' then, perhaps more long suffering.

The children made their own amusement whilst their parents   "gathered knots of may" and played leapfrog or "Oranges and Lemons". When it was time to go home, we were given a present - a doll for the girls and a pop-gun for the boys. It did not occur to me then, that half a century later would question the wisdom of reinforcing male and female roles by these gifts. I do not know whether it influenced our thinking or not, but what I have seen in the world has taught me to hate guns.

Once a year we received a Sunday School Gift which was usually a religious tract on a story with a Victorian moral, but occasionally the Christian element was missing. I was given a small book called 'Three Jolly Playmates' which I read many times. These were the only books we had at home except for the bible, but I treasured those I owned, perhaps because they were so few.

Seventy years on there is much talk about the so-called decline in reading standards, but I can only state that in the many small, rural Lincolnshire schools which I attended, I was one of the few children who could read well and was often "employed" by the teachers, as a monitor to help the majority who could not. This may have been a good thing for those children and for teachers, but I have often thought that I should have been encouraged to continue my own studies.

Chapter 7
"Workhouse Brat"

The work on the water boring had been completed at the moated farmhouse. A water wheel and pump had been installed. My stepfather operated the pump as part of his casual labour every day for a fortnight to clear the water until it ran clear. It was then that he started to tell us he "could see different things at once".

On New Year's Eve he did not go to work as he felt so unwell, suddenly complained of a blinding head ache and collapsed. I ran to the top farm to get help and two of the workmen came back with me. My stepfather became violent and then men had to hold him down in bed while I fetched the doctor. This meant walking five miles as there was no transport or telephone. When I returned with the doctor three hours later, he told my mother that Tom had had some sort of fit or stroke, but he was calmer by then. His speech was affected for many years after that. We lived on Lloyd George sick pay which was just a few shillings. After three or four weeks, Dad was no better and a second doctor told mother than he would have to go into hospital. For people like us, that meant the infirmary at the Workhouse. The tied cottage we lived in belonged to the farmer who was on the Board of Governors of Caistor Workhouse and he arranged for us all to be admitted. I am not sure whether it was out of sympathy so the family could be together, or because a replacement labourer needed the cottage.

The day soon came for us to leave. A taxi arrived and I was very excited at the prospect of a ride in such an unfamiliar form of transport. However, I was most upset at the thought of leaving behind my pet ginger cat Kelly, even though the farm foreman said that he would be alright living in the barn with the mice. I thoroughly enjoyed the twelve mile journey and it was not until the taxi turned unto the drive of a huge building, that I panicked about prospect of living in the Workhouse.

My stepfather was taken to the Infirmary area and my mother was set to work in the kitchens directly. Tom, my stepbrother, and me were taken by the House Mistress to a bathroom and told to wash ourselves thoroughly. Afterwards she checked for lice and behind our ears. Tom had to repeat the wash. She sorted out brown corduroy suits for each of us which didn't fit very well. Next we were led to one of three wards where a lot of old and - to us - funny men were just sitting. On the floor there were spittoons with sawdust in for them to spit in, which they often did.

At five o'clock we were taken to a large Dining Hall, where the Warden, dressed in a black uniform, stood in a pulpit mumbling prayers and grace. All the male inmates were there including about five boys. Tea consisted of two large rounds of bread each with a pat of margarine and a big enamel mug of weak tea.

We went to bed quite early in a large dormitory with lots of old men. The next morning we were shown again where to wash and trooped into the Dining Room where breakfast was again bread, marge and tea.

A Workhouse Board of Governors about 1920

On the following day I was sent to school in Caistor about half a mile way from the Workhouse. Stepbrother Tom, who had left school, had to work in the institution laundry to earn his keep. I went back for dinner with the other Workhouse brats. The men ate at 11.30 and had left the Dining Hall by the time we got there. The food was truly awful, even to a lad like me used to poor meals. On Monday it was a boiled beef with sloppy veg. We never had puddings. Tuesday it was the same, Wednesday bread and cheese, Thursday an enamel mug of what they called soup, Friday a sort of meat and Saturday soup again.

Soon we were put in a ward with men who were a bit more respectable. In the evenings they played cards amongst themselves whilst the boys played 'Drink the Well Dry'. We made so much noise that they threatened us with all sorts of punishments if we did not shut up.

Once a week we were allowed to see my mother and father. We would be taken to meet my mother at the women's ward entrance and visit Tom in the infirmary. This was always on Sunday afternoons. We looked forward to it very much and it was very hard when the time came to go back to our own dormitory for another week.

Sometimes you felt really hungry at night. One young man who had T.B. was specially allowed a mug of Quaker Oats which he would often give to me. I felt very grateful. One night my stepbrother told me he was scared because the men in the next bed to him said Tom snored and had threatened to smother him with his pillow. Being the braver of the two, I told the warden and he had the man moved to another ward.

Whilst it was grim there the other lads and me managed to have some fun as children will in most circumstances. After school and at weekends we would roam around the sewerage farm and in the vegetable plots. We used to play games in the big woodyard where casual vagrants had to saw and chop firewood. I well remember an old basket invalid chair in which we pushed one another around, until one day we travelled so fast that we crashed into a wall and 'bust it'. Of course "We didn't do it". Since no one else knew, it was left like that.

In the workhouse the men received an ounce of tobacco a week. My Dad was a non-smoker and made a few coppers by selling his ration. Every inmate got one shilling a month pocket money and the children sixpence.

Later in our stay we began to have an egg a few times a week for tea. I often wonder if some official complained about our poor diet. Mine was improved by one old boy who sat opposite me at mealtimes. He had no teeth. He used to soak his bread in his mug of tea and give me his pat of marg. I was doing alright!

School was a break from the Workhouse routine, but the Caistor one was much larger than I had come across in the villages. It had a sports field where we were taken twice weekly. I was chosen to play football and was useless as the other schools were too small to raise a team. I begged to play rounders instead but the Headmaster made me play full back. It was a thrill to be told by the other lads that I had played a marvellous match as we

Workhouse boys were teased constantly about our home and usually were the ugly ducklings.

My stepfather slowly became stronger and after three months we were able to return home to Buslingthorpe. My time in the workhouse left an impression on my young mind which was to remain with me throughout my life. It influenced my outlook and helped form my political views.

I was overjoyed to find my cat Kelly safe in the barn at home and he seemed pleased to see me again too. Perhaps there was justice in the world.

Chapter 8
"Learning by Billiard Cue"

When I started back at my old school in Faldingworth, the Headmaster quizzed me so much in front of the class about my time in the workhouse that I could have cried. "What was the food like? What were the people like in there? Did I see my parents often? etc. etc." However he was a man I really liked and I don't think his intentions were unkind. He simply wanted the other children to learn about life in the institution.

Admission Register at Faldingworth School of Fred (known then as Lilley)

It was a good school run by him and his two daughters. The boys had a small plot of ground each to grow vegetables on and we used to take home carrots, peas, beans, lettuces and radishes. My mother was very pleased to receive them. He read lots of books to us like "Uncle Tom's Cabin", "Tarzan of the Apes" and my favourite "Coral Island". I have never forgotten the story to this day. He read and we learnt many poems my heart. "The Ancient Mariner", "Horatio Kept the Bridge" and "The Lady of Shallot" are classics I remember from those days.

The Head kept order with his voice and a shortened Billiard cue. If we were not paying attention, he would come up behind us and rub hard behind our ears with the end of the cue. This really hurt. However we accepted the need to maintain discipline one way or another. To me, he seemed quite nosy, and would ask us what we were having for Christmas Dinner. I said, "Turkey", but we actually had rabbit stew, my stepfather being ill and so poor. In fact we had quite a few free rabbits, thanks to the cat Kelly who would bring home quite big specimens on his nights out. I always demanded the rabbit head at such feasts because I loved the tongue and the brains. Later in life I felt I had missed out. There would have been far more meat on a leg than breast.

Mr Davey, the Headmaster, took us for mental arithmetic. I loved it. The boys would sit or stand in a line and have to answer questions very quickly. If you gave the correct answer you moved up above all those who had not responded successfully. He used to give a penny for each right answer which was a great incentive to me then, but in later years I thought how unfair this competitive system was for the less able lads in the class.

Extracts from Faldingworth School Log Book 1920

Another of his schemes was to allow the boy who answered a particularly difficult question to leave the school ten minutes early. This meant on one occasion, I managed to reach the copse of a walnut tree one windy day before any other boy. I collected seventy nuts that day. The copse belonged to a farmer from a neighbouring village who arranged to visit the school to inspect hands for the telltale stains. Fortunately I had gone home to dinner.

On special religious days we had to go to church from school, and the parson was an old devil. He insisted that when we entered the church we were absolutely spotless and our boots polished and shining. We dreaded it, because the cart tracks and farm gates on our way to school were so muddy. The beasts made them like that. We tried desperately to clean off our boots by taking them off and wiping them on the long grass, but it did not work very well.

Near the school was a pond containing lots of newts. We used a worm and a pin to catch them. Some of the newts had yellow and black markings on their bellies, which Mr.Davey told us were the Great Crested variety. I have learnt recently that they are only found in fairly flat areas and are becoming rare. We never gave a thought to the idea that one day they might become scarce.

Stepbrother Tom bought home eight shillings a week from his work, which helped to supplement father's sick pay, so we had a little more to spend at the village shop. This smelt of so many things. If we had a penny we could buy a ha'penny worth of dates and some thing called "locus beans" which were a kind of pressed animal feed. This was part of a sheep and cattle food. Sometimes we bought boiled sweets, nine-a-penny, or caramels four-a-penny. At about this time the shop started selling "pop". We always went for the cherry flavour, a very sickly drink. Occasionally we ran errands for a neighbour and earned a copper or two to spend on such treats. The village bakery was housed in the corn mill which still ground the corn and sold 'four pound tin' loaves.

At this school there were four boys who were real bullies to us younger ones, and since I had not experienced such behaviour in any of the other schools I learnt to fight like all the others out of necessity. Probably because of my Italian ancestry, I had a rather prominent Roman nose which bled easily. This meant that I nearly always lost these battles, but I never understood why one school had bullies and others escaped. Faldingworth certainly was a more competitive place, so perhaps that had something to do with it. However, the headmaster was a jolly sort of man and during the holidays used to work in the harvest fields with the labourers and us lads. He joined in with all the rough banter and none of us looked on him as the Schoolmaster then.

My Cub Scout neckerchief was a proud possession when I joined Tenderfoot. I loved the organised paper trails and pack activities arranged for us. Unfortunately, the troop was disbanded after some older boys caused trouble at the Vicarage! There have always been yobs who spoiled it for the majority.

Here I earned my shilling a day once more, minding the cows in the lanes. The very wide grass verges, so unlike the steep hedgebanks which I learnt to love in my Devon Retirement, were alive with butterflies - small blues, yellows and browns as well as the larger species. Old fashioned bumble bees buzzed in the masses of ladies' fingers, primroses, violets and bluebells which thrived there in those unpolluted spring days.

The wild dog rose climbed up nearly every hedge in June. I do not think I am seeing this memory through "rose-coloured spectacles". Because of the removal of many hedgerows and the use of pesticides in recent years, I am sure there are less wild flowers. My favourite was, and still is, the beautiful primrose. To see them near the banks of a stream early on a dewy morning, is something you never forget. The heavenly smell of bluebells waving in the woods cannot be described. If, while tenting cattle we had young calves with us, I would do my best to ride on their backs. One day a local farmer spotted me. I got a right telling off and threatened with the sack, which would have meant losing my precious shillings. I gave up my bucking bronco act, but I think I was just a normal country lad of my time and class.

If anything could be eaten in the lanes and field, I found it. As well as raiding crops like peas, broad beans, swedes and turnips, I used to enjoy blackberries and sloes which were very bitter and raw mushrooms. We all instinctively knew the poisonous fruits and plants. Even the rose briar was tempting. You had to peel down the sweet briar and suck it.

Chapter 9
"Bikes, Puttees and Nits"

Stepfather Tom was still a long way from being fit and light farmwork was not often available. He suffered another slight stroke which made the position even worse. Next Lady Day he was given notice and we had to move yet again, this time to a house at Newton Toft about six miles away near Rasen. This semi-detached cottage had a crown stamped on the wall and signified, I was told later, that it belonged to Government or Royalty. We were allowed to stay there even though Tom managed only occasional casual work. I suppose it was an early form of 'Council' housing.

The village setting was marvellous. At the centre was the green with its large, round, duck pond. On one side was the school playground. Opposite stood the church and a row of lovely copper beeches next to a large grass mound. In the far corner near a copse were the farmhouse buildings and orchard. Later I was to be Groom Boy there.

Whoever planted the orchard certainly understood what they were doing. Early apples were followed by the delicious and now rare Russets. Victoria and Greengage Plums mingled with damsons, cherries early and late gooseberries, red and blackcurrants and even cob nuts.

The little school had only thirty pupils aged five to thirteen and we were all housed in one classroom. I was well pleased to find one of my pals from a previous school there. We used to watch the wild life from the school windows. It was all part of practical education. In the Spring you could see the blue tits feeding their offspring who were on parade on the clothes line. The parent popped the collected food into the eager young beaks, always in turn it seemed, making sure each got their fair share. Often we had lessons on the bank under the copper beeches. The four geese would join us but were always rather aggressive. The calves looked ok and we thought they wanted to join in. Once a week we went for 'nature walks'. Whilst we enjoyed these immensely, we knew that we had to write a letter about our observations when we returned. Woe betide us if we did not write a good one!

It was at this point that I concluded that all girls were stupid. Happily this proved to be a passing phase. On wet weekends we lads used to play in the farm barn and usually one or two girls would be there. We played games connected with the farm, as one might expect. We would pretend the waggoners were taking the 'thrashed' corn into town and each person in turn had to think of something useful which might be brought back on the empty wagon. The one who could not think of a sensible item was out. The boys would keep going for a long time but these girls found it hard to manage round one and always ended up repeating what a boy had said. If I suggested three ton of coal so would they. However I soon learnt that girls could be just as bright! My prejudice did not last long.

That summer the Vicar bought a football and a set of cricket gear to school. We never had enough boys to form a team, so condescendingly, we would stick three or four girls in goal. All the lads thought it was hilarious as the girls fell back on their arses screaming, when we kicked the ball at them really hard.

Once I watched some older boys pee all over some apples and make girls eat them. Teenagers have always had nasty traits!

There was no school uniform but I do not think it made any difference to our behaviour. The boys usually wore rough trousers buttoned at the knee and a jacket with a collar fastened with a red ribbon. In the winter the trousers were mostly corduroy.

The First World War puttees had just appeared in the second hand shops. These were strips of material wound around the legs and our parents found that one puttee cut in half was sufficient to wind round our legs to keep out the cold and wet. The 'legging' was wound over heavily nailed and toe capped boots - the forerunners of Doc Martens.

We left school about three o'clock in the winter, having less dinner time to allow us to get home before dark. No lifts home or school buses in those days, just muddy cart tracks to trudge through. I would look forward to a basin of hot bread and milk or sometimes rabbit broth if the 'poacher' had been successful.

The world opened up for me when I learnt to ride my Mother's bicycle. It was the typical 'sit up and beg' model, and since I could not reach the seat I stood on the pedals. There were no brakes. Who needed brakes anyway? It was pretty flat country and you could only hit a horse and cart. I was able to cycle into Market Rasen five miles away and see that big world out there.

One day the farm foreman's wife said that her son had outgrown his bike and it was for sale. She wanted £1 for it. If only I could find the money it would be bliss. I used to take her money when ever I could from the little I earned or scrounged. When I had reached twelve shillings Tom was taken ill again. There was no money at all at home and no income support! That morning, without telling my mother, I set off to ask for my bike money back. 'Alright' announced the farm woman, 'no money, no bike'. Having collected my mother's cycle, I rode into town and bought groceries, bread and meat. On my return my mother wept. I never did get my bike. We had food for another week but we lived on scraps for a long time after that. The headmaster noticed how undernourished I must have looked, and when the local doctor came to school I was called in and examined. After that every dinner time I had to go to the School House for a mug of sweet cocoa. Even now I get angry when I hear about modern politicians carping about the welfare state. Those in need should be provided for. We must not return to the conditions of my youth.

Victoria Jubilee with the sit-up-and-beg

Shortly afterwards the district nurse came to the school to examine our heads for lice. She told me I had nits and the neighbours' children said I was lousy.

My mother started a row and the other woman joined in eventually hitting her calling her 'a blackheaded bugger'. She had an abundance of blue/black wavy hair which was very thick, just like mine and probably like my Italian grandfather. I'm ashamed to admit that I was too cowardly to try to stop the woman from hitting my mother. Nits have always roused passions and prejudices amongst children and parents and only very recently has the stigma been removed since lice prefer clean hair. However, despite modern treatments, headlice are still common, I'm told.

That year the Vicar bought an ex-army hut for £100 on site. This was brought to the village and assembled as a social centre. For the Grand Opening the School organised a concert as part of the event. We rehearsed for weeks. The girls were to perform various dances wearing crowns and paper flowers - Japanese style, and right Prima Donnas they proved to be. Four of us lads were chosen to sing 'D'yeken John Peel'. We were to sing a verse each, but it was like the old Sunday School recitations all over again. Were those loud precocious lads out in the playground the same as those uttering such weak tomorrows? It was decided that we should sing together.

It was a proud night. The school performed in the first half to thundering applause and after the interval a man played the concertina whilst another did a clog dance. Lastly the adults danced the Roger De Coverley and other favourites. The entertainment was followed by minced corned-beef sandwiches and cakes and my mother was not too proud to take home lots of offered 'doggy bags'.

The Vicar, who had a laugh like Edward Heath, had guffawed all evening. We used to mock him behind his back, but we knew he helped the village greatly by his efforts.

Chapter 10
"Two Shillings For Mablethorpe and Five Bankrupts"

Later, that summer, our caring parson arranged 'A trip to the seaside'. Most of the village children had never seen the sea even though it was only twenty miles distant, so the preparations caused great excitement and anticipation. We talked for days about what it would be like and what we would do there.

An open lorry was hired for the outing and we helped load on board the Sunday School benches. To us this was luxury travel, but now the law would forbid it! One kind farmer -there were a few- promised a shilling for each child, which meant that I had a total of two shillings to squander.

As we set out for Mablethorpe we might just as well have been heading for foreign climes. We chatted about what we had bought for dinner. I was well pleased with my hard boiled egg and piece of Madeira cake. We gabbled on about how we would spend our money.

On arrival the sea was a revelation to us. We paddled nearly all day not thinking how we would get dry. The adults had to work hard to persuade us to leave the beautiful briny. I bought a bucket and spade and caught a small crab to my delight. Needless to say 'Fearless Fred' later climbed up the Pier structure and had to be rescued from the in-coming tide. The remainder of our pocket money went on donkey rides and an icecream and tea was provided in the cafe. Fishermen were selling masses of plaice and dabs - a bagful for a shilling. When it was time to go home, I insisted on taking the dead crab which, in the heat of the day, stank to the dismay of the adults on the lorry. The vicar took us on a conducted tour of the local churches on the way home, which did not greatly impress us lads, but our first visit to the seaside made a lasting impression -a rare view of a world outside our parochial lives.

Another first for me was the annual fair in Market Rasen. We walked the five miles into town and there were the sights and smells unknown to me. Roundabouts, swingboats and a cat walk vied for my attention with the Aunt Sally stalls. You had to throw wooden balls at the long rag dolls fixed on racks. If you managed to knock the dolls back, you won a prize. I soon learnt the fairground men were very cunning, particularly with the coconut shies. Rarely did anyone succeed in dislodging a coconut from its support. The pony and donkey rides were less interesting to us farm lads since we were still living in the horse transport age. This event was also a horse fair when horses were sold. The dealers would run up and down trying to show off their animals to the best advantage. We thought the tubes filled with water which young men bought to squeeze over girls were great fun and wished we could join in.

Near the fair was a fish and chip shop and for the first time in my life I sampled the delight of buying two pennyworth of chips that dinnertime. It was a never to be forgotten experience.

It was haircut time and the barber's Brilliantine spray which tried to order the parting in my mop of unruly hair, made me feel very grown-up. Vainly I hoped that passers-by would look at me as we wearily trudged the five miles home.

A neighbouring Vicar visited our school to give a talk on 'Wild Birds'. He arranged an egg collecting competition with prizes, a practice which would be met with horror by teachers and environmental experts nowadays. He did urge us to take only one egg from a nest, but what do you do if there are only four eggs and four boys? You each take one! An old clock case I found proved a useful display cabinet, when fitted with partitions and lined with moss. My favourite egg was a kestrel's which I discovered in a crow's nest. Our method of blowing eggs meant making a small hole at one end and a slightly larger one at the other and blowing hard. Sometimes we managed to suck out the contents which tasted quite good, particularly the thrush and blackbird. I thought my collection was impressive but I did not win. We never gave a thought to conservation, but nor did anyone else.

Pets have always been important to me and even as a child in a rough, country community, I was easily upset if harm came to them. It was around this time that our cat, Kelly, disappeared. I was very sad but the farm foreman told us that he had seen him wild in the woods. We saw or heard nothing for months until one October day he strolled into the house as though he never left. He evidently preferred to hunt for food rather than rely on the scraps we could afford to give him. In the following Spring he left for the woods again, a ritual he observed three years running.

Two 'old' ladies had come to live in a new bungalow in the village. Anyone over forty was old! One day we found a dead cat in the churchyard hedge and guessed correctly that it might belong to the old dears. We arranged the burial for them right away and started digging the grave. When it was judged deep enough, poor Pinky was wrapped in a blanket and laid to rest with due ceremony and affecting lamentations.

The ladies gave us cups of tea and sixpence each which we gratefully accepted. I am embarrassed to recall that our sad thoughts about Pinky were soon replaced by group plans for spending our reward. We had a passion for smoking and were often allowed to collect cigarettes from the shop for farm men. So it was nothing for us to ask for three packets of Woodbines for Bill Tindalls or Charlie Chambers. We smoked like factory chimneys on our way home from school through the fields, boys and girls.

A man came to live next door as a clerk of works. It turned out that he forged cheques to pay local tradesmen and cleared off to London where he was arrested. It's strange that after all these years I remember his name - Cyril Holland Smith. He was gaoled for eighteen months. A puppy called Spike was abandoned at the house and we adopted him. He gave us lots of fun, but some time later we had to sell him as we could not afford to feed him properly. We never received the five shillings we were owed and learnt that he became quite savage with his new 'owners'.

My pride was hurt at the annual sports day that year. In the wheelbarrow race I had to partner with the local farmer's daughter. When she took hold of my legs she noticed my old patched trousers and dropped my legs like a hot cake. I was very hurt and to this day I still have a chip on my shoulder. The snobbery in the farmer's daughter was class distinction personified.

There were at least five bankrupt farmers in our area. I remember that the Bailiffs had seized two wagons from one in particular, which were put up for auction in Rasen for non payment of rates. The other farmers refused to buy the wagons and they were sold for three and sixpence and then returned to the original owner. The drays must have been worth £20 or £30 each, but mother said that farmers supported their own class. I realise now that it could be seen as loyalty.

In those days it was common practice for farmers to have the poultry and some beasts put in their wives' names to prevent the stock being confiscated. Another ploy was to drive the bullocks and sheep to friendly farmers a few miles away, if they got wind of the bailiff coming. When the farmer was declared bankrupt, he usually stayed on as tenant as the new owner could not allow the land to become derelict or scrub. I remember that all the gossips believed that Buchy Barron, Fussey, Tim Inman, Parby and Bishet went that way. This wholesale bankruptcy was caused by new Government taxes. The farm labourers also lost their jobs or received an even smaller pittance in wages. So what's new?

Some of the more 'progressive' farmers started leaving some arable fields to be ploughed by cultivator instead of horses. As lads we loved these engines. Two were used, one on each side of the field. Attached to each was a large drum with a very strong steel cable and in between a large plough with twelve plough shares. These were so arranged that half were upended while being pulled to one side of the field, and then the other side was pulled down.

This continued until about six furrows had been completed and then the engines moved the breadth of the ploughing and began the process again. This method allowed a large field to be ploughed in one day.

Chapter 11
"Champings, Lambings and Bislings"

Our house was part of a farm estate called Doglands. A mile-long cart track with axle-deep ruts led to it from the nearest road. The farm belong to a fishing trawler owner who lived on the coast, and was managed by the farm Bailiff. It consisted of eight heavy horses, beasts, sheep, poultry, grassland, some arable, and meadows together with a large woodland area. Near our house were three large grass fields know as 'The Three Pips". Each had a pond. In the summer the horses were let out to graze after their work. They used to walk down the track at a very leisurely pace sedately by an elderly Roan called Strawberry. She never allowed the frisky ones -Violet, Blossom, Daisy, Prince, Jerry and Thomas- to get in front and was always on top of the pecking orders. The Head Waggoner was always given first choice of the horse team - a pair.

Once when I was helping to lead Prince from stook to stook during harvesting, I thought he was a bit sluggish, so I gave him a slap. Was he on his metal all that day! Prince nearly pushed the man off his wagon as he slashed the sheaves. The worker boxed my ears and threatened dire consequences if it happened again. In my old age I have a china horse which I sentimentally named after Prince.

In winter the horses were kept in the stables. Another boy and I would join the single waggoners in the evenings and play cards there. We sat on the large corn and chaff bins. The heat from the stable lanterns and the eight large horses tempered the cold nights. It was a delight to hear the loud champings and occasional snorts as the horses ate their meal of oats, beans and watered chaff.

There were various categories of skilled trades on the farm, but during hay or corn harvest everybody mucked in. One or two men were hired to stack and thatch the corn stacks. Eighteen stone sacks of corn had to be carried from the thresher to the barn or loading wagons. Cows had to be milked, lambs reared, turnips and swedes gathered and sheep transferred to the swede fields, which were then sectioned by wire netting so nothing was wasted. In the lambing season the shepherd had a large hut on wheels which housed a stove. He stayed there all night, emerging only to check the sheep for signs of lambing. Another of the shepherd's skills was to make hurdles from hazel branches spliced with straw and evergreens. These were used as windbreaks to protect the new-born lambs.

There were always jobs to be done on the farm. On wet days the men would wind long balls of tarred string around short sticks in such a way that the thatcher could unwind it easily for use. There was cotton and seed slabs of cake to be fed into the big grinder ready for the cattle. Corn sacks needed to be sorted and repaired with a spot of sewing. Soon after lambing, males were castrated and tails were cut. It was my job to go round making sure that any lambs lying down got up. The men said they would bleed to death if I did not, but I never quite believed it. Much spreading took place periodically. My job was to take a full cart-load of manure to the man who was already spreading one load bringing back the empty cart to the men in the crew yard and so on.

Sometimes there would be rows between the workers because those taken on temporarily were on piecework and those regulars in the field were not. I thought it was unfair. However all the men took great pride in their work. The thatcher ensured that each stook was neatly topped and would sometimes put a wooden "COCHLEATE" at the end of each stook. The wagons were loaded carefully in shape and neatness. Even though it was perhaps only half a mile back to the stack yard, it mattered.

Sometimes I accompanied the rabbit catcher. He would tie a cord to a ferret's leg and put it down a rabbit hole, having first covered the other entrances to the warren with nets. The poor terrified rabbits would rush up and were quickly dispatched.

I was inspired by adverts in the local paper which announced that skin merchants were offering five pounds per hundred moleskins. The molecatcher took me out one day. Later I filled a trap and set it near a range of molehills. I had visions of quick wealth, but my dream were frustrated. The traps had to be camouflaged with grass and soil in the tunnels to disguise the smell of human hands. So my first (and not last) get rich scheme came to nought.

The farmer's wife had an important role to play in running the farm. usually she controlled the poultry and the dairy. She organised the butter making. A machine separated the cream from the whey and she had to churn the cream until it changed to butter. The churn consisted of a well-polished barrel attached to a metal frame. In the centre of the barrel were metal bars. The cream was poured in and the lid sealed. The churn was operated by a side handle which was turned at a steady pace. Sometimes the process was over quickly but might take two hours. When it was ready the separated buttermilk was used to feed calves or pigs. The actual butter was weighed in individual pounds, patted into shape and a design marked on top. Finally each pat was wrapped in greaseproof paper and packed ready for the weekly market.

Another task was collecting and counting the eggs for market. Sometimes they would kill and dress the old boiler fowls for display too.

The richer farmers usually employed two maids to help with all these jobs and the housework. There was no collection of milk from the farms as it was normal for local people to bring their own billy can to collect it together with eggs when needed. The milk was not treated in any way but I do not remember anyone being reported ill. Unused milk was fed to the pigs and calves. When a calf was born the mother's milk was was especially thick. It was sweetened and cooked in a deep dish. The result was a sort of custard called locally, bisling or breshings. We thought it tasted really good but I am not sure I would care for it now.

There was always a large orchard and during apple dropping time the pigs were driven in. They soon made short work of the fallen, grub-ridden apples. The apple harvest was a mammoth task which everyone joined in and the crop was carefully stored for the farmer's own use. Whilst the apples had a wonderful taste and were unaffected by chemical sprays, they were often imperfect in shape and scabby looking. They would not have found a place on modern supermarket shelves where shoppers have been trained to expect uniformity.

Chapter 12
"Prime Minister or Old Job Boy"

Word came for me to attend Lincoln City Hospital to have my tonsils and adenoids removed. I was thrilled, not at the prospect of the operation, but by the vision of five weeks off school and missing the dreaded Christmas concert. The teacher quickly shattered that hope by telling me that I would be back at school within a week.

The local carrier's cart, now covered-in, took mother and I the eighteen miles to Lincoln, picking up parcels in each village on this adventure.

I had been warned to consume no food or drink, but when my mother called at a City shop, I nipped next door, bought two sausage rolls and secretly gobbled them. At the hospital a dozen other children awaited a similar fate. At two-thirty the ether-soaked pad was placed over my nose and mouth and shortly the offending appendages were removed. At that time it was very common, but now I think the procedure is much rarer.

We were taken by taxi to an annex run by 'two old dears' and put to bed. The sausage rolls ensured the inevitable bout of vomiting, but I kept the reason quiet, determining not to be so impulsive in future. Needless to say my resolve has often faltered! After a breakfast of porridge none of us wanted, with throats on fire, we were sent on our way. We took the train to our nearest station and walked the remaining five miles home.

The headmaster at Newton Toft suggested that I sit the scholarship entrance examination for The De Aston Grammar School at Market Rasen and so I duly took the mock papers and was told by him that, on that showing, it was highly likely that I would gain a place.

It meant buying books and a uniform and a five mile cycle ride each way winter and summer. I really was desperate to take up this opportunity, but after much discussion with my mother and Tom, it was decided that I should not. They simply could not afford it, since stepfather was often unemployed due to his poor health and there was no dole for farmworkers.

So there went my chance of becoming Prime Minister! Well perhaps not, but certainly had circumstances been different, much of my life might well have been transformed.

Just a week before my thirteenth birthday my schooldays ended.

Four of us left Newton Toft that March; I think to make room for infants in this tiny thirty pupil school. It is ironic that my son ended his career as Head of such a small school in Devon.

The vicar had hoped to have secured me a job as apprentice to the wheelwright and carpenter in the neighbouring village, but that position was taken up by the carpenter's own son.

It was then that my mother had bought me my first pair of long trousers. A friend had been similarly breeched and each time we met each other we doubled up with laughter. When we noticed anyone approaching, we hid. Children now hardly seem to wear short trousers at all.

I started work at the Bailiff's in the village as odd job boy, but preferred to be known as groom boy as it sounded more 'upmarket'. My actual work was cleaning out the animal sheds each day, brushing down the pony and feeding the chickens. But in addition I helped in the scullery peeling potatoes, washing and scrubbing, cleaning knives and forks, boots and shoes. It was my task too, to operate the separator and butter churn once a week.

The Bailiff only kept enough stock to provide food for the family. Extra milk had to be bought for the pigs. A few chickens and ducklings were reared and I had to maintain the coops. I had to make time to chop firewood and help on washing day - always Monday. This entailed dollying the clothes in a galvanised tub. The dolly peg - my son still has one - was like a three-legged stool with a long handle attached. The object was to move the dolly peg up and down and from side to side in the tub working up a lather. Then the clothes were rinsed and put through the mangle with its huge rollers to squeeze out as much water as possible. Before the Bailiff's wife took the clean clothes over to the drying area on the village green, she produced another load for dollying. I was usually so weary that I perched on the edge of the tub until I saw her returning, and then whipped up a good lather.

Keeping the pony trap, an elegant item of transport with rubber tyres, clean and polished was an activity in which I took great pride. They used it to go to market in Rasen once a week. I was well pleased with my first shiny pair of black leggings.

At the end of my first year I received the grand total of four pounds, with a rise of two pounds for the second. Once when my mother asked for a little more money to buy me working clothes he grumbled like fury.

However they did 'feed' me. Breakfast, the only meal, usually meant a thick slice of fat, boiled bacon which my stomach revolted against. Since I ate in the scullery, it was simple to slip it into my pocket. The lucky hens used to run towards me when I went into the crew yard, and instantly devoured the evidence. I went hungry and it is difficult to think how I survived, although I was able to look forward to Sunday dinner at home. To catch the pony I needed an apple or small bran mash and I know I took my share! To make sure you were never idle, you were never allowed to visit the fields without a 'spud'. This was a very small hoe. As you walked you 'spudded' any thistles in your path. This certainly helped to keep these weeds under control.

Chapter 13
"Bailing, Farting and a Rollicking"

For some months my mother had been complaining of severe back pains and was eventually admitted to the City Hospital where she underwent a very serious abdominal operation. It was three weeks before Christmas and the Bailiff grudgingly gave me the day off to visit her.

The only form of transport available for the eighteen mile journey was her bike. The front tyre burst about seven miles from Lincoln. Although I struggled to ride with the flat, I had no option but to push it most of the way. My stepfather's brother had arranged to meet me and as soon as I saw him I was so overwrought that I burst into tears. The thought of having to use money saved to buy fruit or sweets for my mother, to buy a new tyre was too much. My step-uncle took pity on me and made up the difference for the tyre, but mother never got her fruit. The journey home was extremely difficult along the dark country lanes, as the bike lamp kept blowing out.

We had a pretty miserable Christmas. Dinner was spare ribs and dad bought me a printing set.

Although I had reached the argumentative stage, I missed my mother greatly. After what seemed an age she came home by train and pony trap on a bitterly cold day. She was still very ill.

Work at the Bailiff's continued as before with one exception: every Wednesday I had to walk four miles to the home of a relative of the Bailiff's housekeeper to help with the dollying and mangling and chop firewood. Sixpence and a chance to dawdle on the way back lessened this chore, but the work at Doglands still had to be completed on my return.

I have never liked the Shepherd and Sheep Parable since the day the Bailiff ordered me to visit a farm some distance away to count sheep. Having duly counted, with considerable difficulty, seventy sheep and returned with the result he insisted that I go all the way back for a recount. Yes, there now appeared to be seventy one! With practice my system of counting improved, but later I always declared the wretched things were all there.

A bike journey I enjoyed was when I was sent to order the threshing machine for Doglands from a distant farm. Jacko one of the farm dogs raced along with me. One day I hit upon an idea which I thought would save my legs. He was always raring to go, so I attached a rope to his collar and set forth with my patent labour-saving device. Away went Jacko in seconds; so did I, straight over the handlebars. The bike suffered a broken pedal which caused trouble. Only my pride was hurt. After this, Jacko and I kept our energy sources completely separate. He always made it home first, since he used the short cuts across the fields and mum's bike and I had to follow the twisting lanes.

On threshing days the machine would appear rumbling along the cart track and be set up near the stack to be threshed. The engine was placed in position the correct distance from 'the drain'. A man stood on top of this contraption. As the sheaves were thrown down to him by another labourer on the stack, he cut the sheaf twine and fed it into 'the drain'. After much shaking and tossing inside, the threshed corn emerged from one exit and the chaff and straw from the other. The final part of the set-up was the elevator often called the Jack Straws. This stairway-like piece of machinery housed a conveyor belt consisting of several claw-like teeth which transferred the straw on to the stack. The Jack Straw could be adjusted to different heights as the stacks grew.

All these sections of machinery were joined by a very long belt and sets of pulleys connected to a large wheel on the engine. Water had to be carried to the engine to keep the boiler full and coal brought for the furnace. At the same time, eighteen stone sacks were being filled with the corn. A small winding jack was used to raise the sacks to aid the men to place the sacks squarely on their shoulders. Each stack was carried to the barn and counted. It was very important to have a counting system as the waggoners got up to all sorts of tricks to steal a sack for the horses. The rogues would often hide corn sacks amongst the chaff and straw, dig a hole or make a false bottom in the stable corn bin. They were devious!

Us lads stood around the base of the stacks and watched the mice and rats scamper out. Often the poor frightened creatures tore round in circles in a confused state as the dogs chased them excitedly. If the rats emerged a few at a time the dogs usually finished them off, but if they staged a mass breakout then some escaped. The rats scared me, probably because of the reputation attributed to them by the men, but I still had a sneaking sympathy for them in their fate. Sometimes a weasel would dash out and did they smell!

On these days I would trudge home happy with a pocket full of mice for Kelly the cat. There would be lots of sweet tea and sometimes a special treat to eat, perhaps a cake.

Haymaking and the corn harvest were both enjoyable times although my normal work had to be fitted in with this extra work. To be fair, the bosses had to muck in and organise too, as everybody's livelihoods depended on getting the job done whilst the weather was right.

After reaping the hay had to be piled in large heaps. I was ragged by the men since I could not keep up with their rate of work, but the pleasure of this activity outweighed the embarrassment of the men's jibes about my size and strength. The delightful 'smell of the new-mown hay' may be a cliche but it makes it no less true. It was marvellous on a hot day. The large bottles of cold tea with sugar but no milk were relished by us all. It was the men's favourite drink. Rarely did they have beer.

'Us lads' felt very proud sitting on the shafts of the loaded wagon, holding the reins and driving the horses back to the stackyard. On our return to the field for a fresh load, being impulsive youngsters, our driving was often reckless. On one occasion we hit and demolished a gate post. We received a 'rollicking' from the boss. His concern was not for the post damage but for the safety of the horses.

Chastened, we took the job much more seriously in future. We loved the horses and even we realised the economic consequences of the loss of one of these magnificent animals. They were faithful, gentle giants. Not once was I trodden on despite their huge feet. They were so used to the routine, that they anticipated the moment when the harness was to be removed after working all day, bending their head and neck down low so that we could remove the collar, which was heavy and had to be turned around. Their reward was always a 'bailing' of hay.

So the months rolled on and it was the corn harvest.

First two men scythed a four foot strip all around the field so that the horses did not tread on the binders and flatten the corn. Two binders pulled by teams of three shires, cut the crop and bound it into sheaves which were thrown off the machine at intervals. Later the men took great pride in carefully forming the sheaves into stooks and meticulously arranged them in straight, parallel lines. When the stooks were as dry as possible, it was often a race against changing weather to see that "all was safely garnered in".

It was during breaks, when the older farmworkers smoked or chewed thick twist - I tried it once and was sick for days - that I took particular notice of their talk and the crude jokes they told.

One 'game' they played was known as "Farting Dominoes". This consisted of three of them farting in turn, the first announcing, "Can you go Coupland?". Then "Can you go, Lilley?" and Lilley, my stepfather, would perform and continue, "Can you go again Bell?". This musical episode would proceed until Bell, who was usually champion, would conclude, "Can you go?". "No!" being the reply, he would shout in triumph, "Well Domino Chain then!" and produce the loudest fart of all. The men all laughed and we joined in. It was crude but harmless fun in difficult times.

One waggoner, who was "partly dumb and spoke with a broken stutter", would point to one of us lad's private parts and declare that they "were soft as a pound of butter" and to another that his "were like two pounds of butter". We were never quite sure what he meant then.

There are endless expressions for referring to one's bodily functions but when these men disappeared behind the hedges for a pee they used two particular phrases: "I'm just going to strain my 'tatoes", or "I'm off to the coffee shop".

All this and the talk about what they had done and what they would like to do to the maid, when she occasionally brought dinner to the field, were part of growing up. Then it was secretive. Now it is more direct and open. It's probably better the modern way.

The single men lived in at the farm and ate in the kitchen. The head waggoner sat at the head of the table. He 'dished out' the food to the others seated in 'pecking order' and tradition had it that as soon as he had finished eating and left the table, all the rest had to leave too. Consequently, the slow eaters soon learnt to speed up. For supper in winter they were given bowls of bread and hot milk with lumps of bacon fat added.

On the very large farms it was the practice for the farm foreman and his wife to billet the young single men and they were paid accordingly. These workers and maidservants were hired each May in Market Rasen. If someone was leaving he or she received a fortnight's holiday at that time and attended the hiring. When the hiring fee had been agreed the two parties would shake hands. The worker usually received half a crown then, which was known as "a Fastening Penny". This meant the hiring had to be honoured. Although a few tried to claim a 'sub' before the end of the agreed year, this was frowned upon and if you wanted a reference you avoided this practice. It was not until the following year that those 'lucky enough' to be hired received their fee. A common amount for men was forty pounds and for the girls fifteen. So this was your first year; there was no money to spend whatever!

At Doglands there was a large rookery in a long field. There seemed to be thousands and in Spring the landowner would invite friends from Grimsby to a shoot. At the first shot the adult rooks would take off to another wood nearby so it was the youngest birds which could barely fly that were the targets. The 'sportsmen' managed to pick off hundreds of these as the poor 'grounded' creatures sheltered in the foliage. I was led to believe that it was only thighs of these young birds that were used for rook pies, and thought how little meat that would provide. However, my son has since discovered a recipe for Rook Pie in an old copy of 'Mrs. Beeton's Household Management'. That states that the backbone and surrounding flesh, neck and skin should be removed after drawing the bird as most of the flesh and bone has a strong, bitter taste. That does not leave much , so the recipe specifies "6 young rooks" is supplemented by "3/4 pound of rump steak"!

Chapter 14
"Rescue The Perishing"

'The Hut' and Chapel were still the centre of our social activities. During the winter we used the Hut for games. The good old parson had acquired two pairs of boxing gloves which we learnt belonged to the champion of the Indian Army. The older men took great delight in watching the smaller lads try to knock the hell out of each other. The gloves were so heavy that I could hardly lift my arms up. We wore no shield, but just hit each other until we dropped. The men laughed and cheered us on, as though it were the world championship. They called us the Bantam Cocks.

On Sunday mornings I still took my regular seat in church, but it was the Chapel in the evening which was better entertainment, despite the rather grim reputation of Wesleyan Methodism. We elected to sit on the back row with the farm men and sing the Moody and Sankey hymns at the tops of our voices. The sticky caramel toffee which we saved up for these evenings, nearly choked us as we rendered "Will your Anchor Hold?", "In the Land of Beulah", "Rescue the Perishing", "Fight the Good Fight" or "Just as I am". We found it extremely difficult to contain our laughter and dare not look at each other when one particular preacher nick-named 'Funny Kirkham' addressed a packed congregation. His antic in the pulpit, as he danced about like a madman and flung his arms wildly, produced convulsions of laughter in 'us lads' which were only suppressed by the disapproving stares of the Bailiff, as he turned and cocked his good eye on us.

My stepfather, unlike me, treated the Prayer Meetings with great reverence . He would take out a clean white handkerchief from his breast pocket, place it on the floor and kneel down on one knee and begin his prayer. In his choked voice, as a result of his stroke, he usually recited the same text which included the following words: "the drunk may come, the swear may come, but I go to my eternal home".

Mother appeared to have made a good recovery from her illness and we still argued furiously. Tom managed to obtain casual work with the threshing machine and became known locally as the 'chaff carrier'. This was very dirty work and certainly not good for the lungs. Once, when he was walking home from a job, a car carrying four young blades stopped. One handed him fourpence thinking he was a tramp. He told us that he took the money without enlightening his benefactor. The town barber refused to continue shaving him and his short back and sides since he made the towels so grubby and put off other customers.

The second year of hiring at Newton Toft was drawing to a close. It was an event which I viewed with mixed feelings. whilst it had been tough, there had been fun times and the lifestyle, in relation to my age and class in a rural community, was the norm. I was looking forward to receiving my six pounds, but fearful of where I would go and what I would do next..

It was on a rare visit to Lincoln that my mother met by chance a distant relative of the lady who had adopted her years before. He owned a Grocery and Bakery business in nearby Waddington. This chance meeting, on reflection, was to become an important milestone in my life. A week afterwards my mother received a letter offering me a job as general baker's boy with a view to learning the baking and confectionery trade. I was to receive four shillings and sixpence a week and 'live in with all found'. The offer was readily accepted and preparations were made for me to start in seven days. I was fourteen.

My six pounds annual income from Doglands mostly disappeared in one day when I was kitted out in Market Rasen with a suit, shoes, shirt and underwear. I thought I was the "cat's whiskers". I wandered around my old haunts during that week and made a sentimental fuss of Kelly the cat.

The morning dawned when, as I thought, I was to leave our village for ever. The five mile walk to the station was uneventful. Both mother and I were subdued. We had dinner in a cafe - a rare treat - and by the time the train tickets had been obtained my hiring money was now a minus sum! Mother helped out, but I have no idea how.

We were met in Lincoln by my new employers, where mother and I said our farewells, I do not know who was the most apprehensive. The 'Silver Queen' open top double decker bus service completed our journey on its way south. Here I was in this much larger village with its three bakeries, butchers, tailors and drapers. When I returned in the 1970s the sign above the draper's, established in 1860, was still proudly shown. How many villages have those small businesses now?

My new employer, Mr Peatman, whom I judged to be in his early sixties, took great pride in showing me round his little empire. There were three separate shops - Grocery, Baker/Confectioners and Hardware. The smell of the bakery itself lingers with me into old age and contrasted later with that pervading his piggery at the other end of the village.

Mrs. Peatman was small and plump and delighted at the way my mother had helped to rig me up with new outfits. Her son helped her run the bakery department and organised the bread round.

It soon got around the village that Palmers' -their trade name- had a fresh lad. I settled in but often felt desperately homesick at fourteen. Breaking in to a tribe of local lads proved difficult. As always, they were suspicious of any 'intruder', but in the fights which inevitably ensued, my boxing training at the Hut helped me gain their respect after winning a few unofficial bouts. I realised at the time that it was necessary to go through this process, but have never understood why intelligent humans capable of discussion, feel the need to 'protect their territory' by aggression as animals do by instinct.

My job in the bakery was greasing tins and trays - a messy task, but less so than my second responsibility feeding the pigs. It was impossible to avoid soaking my clothes with pig swill as I carried the large buckets from the bakers to the piggery. Fear of the rats, which were plentiful, meant that I never neglected to throw stones to try and scare them off.

When I returned, a change of clothes was essential before setting off with the owner's son on the bread round in one of the villages. The cart was pulled by a faithful blue roan Welsh pony called Taffy. Like many ponies he was quite nervy and the village lads knew it. As we trundled along, the more awkward types would bang anything they could lay their hands on, to make Taffy shy or gallop off. Sometimes they succeeded and the out fit took some holding. I am glad that my granddaughter, Polly, turned out to be so good with horses. About six weeks after my arrival, I wrote home to my mother:

"Dear Mam,

I am getting on alright. I made the plum bread for the Chapel tea yesterday. It is very hot in the bakery and the oven fire burns three ton of coal in two weeks.

Your Loving Son, Fred"

The truth was that I had not made any bread but had prepared the tins, and my assertion about the amount of coal was probably fantasy! However at that age you cannot admit you are not thriving and in control. Anyway I have always had a tendency to exaggerate.

Plum bread is a Lincolnshire speciality which has a unique, delicious spicy flavour but like plum puddings contains no plums. A fruit or bun loaf, greatly inferior, is the nearest you can obtain in the south.

The bakery was very old-fashioned and traditional in its methods. The oven could hold about one hundred large loaves and in addition four huge bun trays. The "firing-up" was very important. The oven was stoked up at one end and fire blazed beneath its floor, across its whole length with the smoke funnelling up a huge chimney in the corner.

In two hours or when the oven temperature was hot enough, it was allowed "to settle". When the fire had stopped smoking the floor of the oven had to be cleaned. This was achieved by attaching a sack to a long pole by a chain, dipping it repeatedly into a bucket half full of water and swirling it over the floor until it was clean. Finally, a pair of bread tins was placed on the peel - a long flat shovel - and positioned in the oven. This process continued until all the loaves had been systematically loaded side by side.

Mr. Peatman was an intensely kind, religious man who would often visit me at the piggery and garden. He usually had bread and cheese secreted in his pocket for me and sometimes "Khali" - a powder which you mixed with water to make a refreshing drink. He loved to see me eat second helpings at the table so from a thin, undernourished lad I grew stronger and soon put on weight.

He was a Chapel worthy and Trustee, attending both morning and evening services. I attended only the Sunday morning ritual. The vicar of Newton Toft had written to ask my employer to "keep an eye" on me in chapel but after the first he left me alone. I was glad about that and continued to enjoy diversions from the tedium of religious rites. My thoughts wandered frequently and my mind was full of fantasies. The choir in procession was led by two extremely stout ladies - 'us lads' used far less polite language to describe them. I imagined them to be very large sheep heading for slaughter on the altar, but I always smiled innocently when I met them outside.

For the next few months, my life in this parochial community continued with little change, but I was beginning to grow up. Mrs. Peatman insisted that I go to the Post Office every Monday to deposit a shilling in my bank book. The villagers began to tell the boss that Fred was well-mannered, obliging, friendly and had a winning smile. My ego rocketed, but I'm not sure this confidence boost really helped my arrogant streak.

Chapter 15
"Living and Dying"

The arrival of the Peatmans' grandson signalled another first for me, - my introductions to the silent movies. He invited me to the pictures in Lincoln and the event meant that I could not stop talking about it for weeks. One epic entitled "Half a Dollar Bill" featured a sailor who coming home on shore leave found a baby on his doorstep, with a note asking to take care of it. Enclosed was a half a dollar bill. Needless to say the film had a strong moral theme with the sailor marrying the mother and "living happily ever after". The other film on the bill was a comedy which was a bit like Monty Python. The chief character was trying to use a water pump in the farmyard and each time he pumped, milk came out of the spout and as he placed the bucket underneath it always seemed to be in the wrong place. We thought this was hilarious but would I find so in my old age?

One day an old friend unexpectedly turned up. It was my mother's sit-up-and beg, so I was mobile again. I learned all the tricks, like riding on the seat facing backwards or keeping only the back wheel on the ground so all those modern youngsters who think that "wheelies" are new should think again. As an adolescent I had become a real exhibitionist. Someone reported that all I did was act stupidly on my bike and advertise a particular brand of hair cream. Indeed at the time I had a shock of black hair which needed something effective to control it. The remedy worked on the hair but not much worked on my behaviour.

On some bread round nights, Peatman Junior and I were late home and as Taffy jogged along pulling the van, which was lit only by two candle lights, we would sing songs, first world war songs to keep our spirits up. My favourite was "The Good Ship Yacky Dicky Dooda" but I couldn't compete with the boss's son who had an excellent tenor voice which must have echoed round the lanes. He had musical talent, was an accomplished pianist, and played the chapel organ.

One Sunday Mr.Peatman was most unusually an hour late for lunch, stating that he had been sitting in the churchyard. I remember noticing quite clearly a strange phenomenon which apparently escaped everyone else. His eyes shone with a pure brilliance After dinner, he excused himself, and went upstairs to the sitting room to rest. This was unheard of as he was such an active person. He sat dozing at the table. I sat near the fire reading and his daughter, who was on a rare visit, in an armchair. Suddenly he let out a loud gasp, and his head fell back. He was dead. This was my first encounter with human death but as a young lad I was particularly upset because that very morning he had cause to give me a telling-off for over sleeping and not being there for work. He told me that I would never make a business man. I have never forgotten it and he was proved right.

Death brings changes and since the son had to take full responsibility for the business, it meant that I really did begin baking, unlike my earlier boast, and took on some of the deliveries on my own. Perhaps Mr. Peatman did me a final good turn.

His son became more ambitious and decided to re-start a round which was abandoned during the war. Taffy became so used to our normal runs that he always stopped at customers' houses without any instruction. On our first day with the revised round we were amazed that, even after a lapse of nine years, he stopped at all the old points almost automatically. I thought elephants never forgot!

Local firms took their turn in baking "the poor bread". Every Saturday we distributed it to the known poor and elderly in the village. An anonymous benefactor left provision for it in his will. This practice died out as social conditions improved, but I suspect that it will be revived out of necessity as welfare systems are threatened by right-wing policies towards the end of the century.

Peatmans catered for Sunday School parties from Lincoln each year when they organised sports in one of the nearby fields. We provided a couple of stalls selling ice cream and sweets. We made the ice cream which was more like a creamy custard. The mixture was placed in a narrow, tall container which fitted into a machine and alternate layers of ice and salt were packed around the container. The tedious job of turning the machine handle at a steady pace lasted about a half an hour when the ice cream was ready for sale. The outing organisers brought their own food and tea-making facilities.

Occasionally the local butcher hired one of the Peatman's pig sties. A lad who worked for him called Dab and I had to boil the big potatoes in the copper in the garden. It wasn't only the pigs which had a good meal from them. We dipped them in salt. One of our jobs was to drive pigs to the slaughterhouse a couple of streets away. A particularly large white refused to cooperate and kept turning back. Can you blame it! An old chap looking on announced knowingly "You'll never get him that way. Go and get a brush a yard or two in front of him and let him smell it." That poor pig went straight to his end without a problem. Those old countrymen had passed no exams, but could teach those with paper qualifications a trick or two!

Chapter 16
"Lying, Lusting and Moulding"

I now received a rise of six shillings a week. Such riches.

One afternoon whilst on the round, we were coming out of a farm track with Taffy and the van. Near the gate were two girls. Young Mr.Peatman, who knew them, told me they were taking their father's tea to the harvest field. I thought they were rather pretty and put on my most winning smile. Sylvia, the younger by three years attended Waddington School and apparently later boasted that she had "met the new lad at Peatmans". They lived in Harmston a mile distant along 'The Ramper'. It was Phyllis , the smaller one, that I really noticed.

Mr. Peatman was courting a young War Widow and to my surprise they arrived one evening accompanied by Phyllis, who turned out to be her cousin. Fate had taken a hand in shaping my destiny.

Fred and Phyllis as teenagers

Phyllis and I kept smiling at each other. We said little. The hard-headed cynics of today will dismiss as romanticised cant the notion that I was captivated by her pretty heartshaped face and petite figure; that one moonlight night I kissed her on the cheek and she, gazing upwards, said, "Look at the stars." Mills and Boon stuff, but nonetheless sincerely-felt innocent love which appears no longer to exist.

I saw her again and plucked up courage to ask her to meet me. We arranged to meet on "The Ramper" with two of her friends. They would walk on in front. This happened many times after that and I always bought her a quarter of sweets or chocolates. I would never have one myself.

Attendance at church on Sundays was still part of village life for all. At the end of the service in Waddington and a mile long walk, the tryst took place outside Harmston Church. As the nights drew in that year, I decided to miss the service to get there early.

The Sunday evening ritual began when Mrs. Peatman asked me to set the new crystal wireless set. This early radio had a limited range and was very unreliable. You poked the piece of rock crystal with a short piece of wire and "twiddled" your earphones until you found the best sound. Even the best was very crackly and often faded. On Sundays it was always the bells from St. Martins in the Fields or Crowland Abbey relayed from Chelmsford. Afterwards she regularly complained that I had not set it up correctly, but the slightest vibration would affect the sound. Now we take stereo sound and more for granted, but to us the idea was incredible.

Before I set off "for church" Mrs P. never failed to ask me to check that her elderly Aunt Sally was in the congregation and quite well. Not once did I put in an appearance at the Service that winter, but I always reported she was present and healthy. Sally never let me down! The only tricky question concerned the content of the sermon, but I invariably announced that I could not remember or did not understand the vicar.

One Sunday it happened. Phyllis told me she had a new job and was going away. She had been working at the rectory, but was to become a nanny to the rector's three children on the estate village of a duke. The Duke of Devonshire and Chatsworth meant nothing to me then; Phyllis was leaving. We parted with a kiss and tears. Boys weren't supposed to weep then.

Gloom and despair set in. Yet, as with youth at any time, the pain soon fades. I had to be back with the boys again. Other girls did not interest me. A letter arrived from Phyllis about a month later announcing that she was happy. The children were often naughty but she enjoyed harnessing the pony and trap for rides around the Estate and beautiful grounds.

So, she didn't need me. It was the last letter I received from Chatsworth. "What did I care?"

The trouble is I did! From then on she became known as Miss Phyllis Hard-To-Get.

It was 1924. I was becoming bored by my work at Peatmans and saw an advert in the Lincoln evening paper: "WANTED Young man to work in

Bakery with Bread Rounds. Must be fond of horses".

I learnt that the pay was twenty-five shillings a week, so I took the job. After paying for my digs, which I found locally, that left me with five shillings for clothes and entertainment.

During the interview the Boss and the Head Baker asked if I could mould dough. Needless to say, I boasted that I could. "One in each hand", I declared, "and I can mix of course".

The moment of truth came when I started work a week later at six a.m. The Head Baker watched my efforts at moulding, whilst the other youth sniggered in the background. I just did not know what to say, but had to swallow my pride and admit that I had lied to get the post. Luckily the Boss still kept me on and I redeemed myself a little during the bread round, when the son reported that I "was very polite to the customers". Things improved. I learnt a lot about the baking trade and not to be so arrogant. Really it was an inferiority complex. I stayed for two years.

Jerry, the Bread Round horse, was a lovable old rogue. He had been kicked out of the Yeomanry because he was too troublesome. someone had only to pass by carrying a bag of cabbages - or indeed any sort of bag - and he would lunge out and grab it. Once settling a shop bread account, I noticed a small boy leaving the shop carrying a straw bag full of vegetables and bread. When I returned to Jerry and the van outside, there in the gutter lay the knotted handle of the bag and a few onions. There was no sign of the boy but I can't believe Jerry had eaten him too!

On another occasion near Stonebow, Jerry the rogue caught his foot in the tramlines on the road nearby and fell down. There were loaves and cakes all over the road with trams, bells clanging, queueing to rattle on past this busy spot. With two bleeding knees, Jerry lay there still attached to the van. Eventually, a few sympathetic men helped me to persuade the horse to get up. Then we all re-loaded the van. Jerry suffered no lasting damage, but always had to wear felt-lined leather kneepads afterwards.

On the Round, after about thirty calls, I used to sit in the van and do the paperwork. It was my custom then to give Jerry a stale cake or bun. Sometimes I would forget to give him the signal with the reins to trot on. He would place his feet firmly on the ground and refuse to budge until I produced the cake.

One Saturday I was driving him through the city centre, when the police stopped the traffic for a long Temperance Procession with all its banners and the band playing rousing marches. As soon as Jerry heard the music he danced and plunged about, presumably remembering his days with the Yeomanry - a volunteer calvary unit. Two or three willing spectators had to help me cover his head and hold him steady until the procession had passed.

One afternoon Jerry and I were stopped by the Weights and Measures Inspector. He forced me to drive to the Sessions House where he weighed all my loaves. Sixty-five out of the seventy were short weight. The bread had been a bit over-baked that day unfortunately. There was nothing deliberate about it. The Boss was taken to court, fined a shilling a loaf and was given a stern public warning.

I enjoyed living and working in the City even though the Bakery hours were long. There were no "Trade Board" wages in those days in the baking world. Having purchased a tailor-made suit, new shirt, patent toe-capped shoes and a natty little trilby hat, as well as a bowler, I thought myself quite the dandy at sixteen. Since I was usually broke, I used the Landlady's clothing club to buy the outfit at half a crown a week. I made an arrangement with he landlady that if I did the washing up, she would knock a couple of shillings or so off the rent.

On Wednesdays afternoons I used to go the pictures. It cost threepence (3d.) for the matinee and, since the programme was continuous, I often stayed until ten o'clock at night. If I could avoid the usherettes noticing me, I would sneak into the better seats during the intervals.

We had a choice of Picture Houses, the Theatre and Variety Palace and on Saturday evenings, when I had time off and any money, I thought I was very grown-up watching the latest thing and catching the last bus home to the digs.

Chapter 17
"Miss Phyllis Harder-To-Get"

And what of Miss Phyllis-Hard-To-Get? Eventually I heard that she was home from Chatsworth, and as a shot in the dark I wrote and asked her if she would like to bring her sister, Sylvia, to Lincoln Fair. To my surprise and delight a reply arrived saying that they would meet me on the Saturday evening. A friend came with me and we all had a jolly evening. I had little money for rides even though they only cost twopence each.

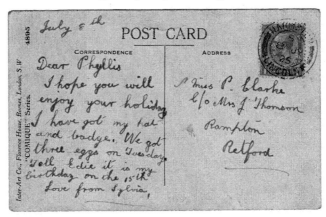

Sylvia sends card to Phyllis who was staying with her older sister Edith

We saw them off on the train. I was a very happy young man and still impressed by Phyllis who was just as pretty and growing up, but I held back from arranging to see her again as I really could not afford to meet her or take her out.

I loved Lincoln with its castle and magnificent cathedral and the bands playing in the parks and that was all free! However one Bank Holiday I decided on the spur of the moment to visit Harmston where Miss Phyllis Hard-to-get lived. The village was famed for its Annual Show and the Major who lived in the Hall and was the local Squire. There was always a cricket match in the morning and then the Flower Show plus a parade by the Hunt with the Hounds. The Horse show and Gymkhana seemed to me a big event. The day always drew a large crowd with the usual sideshows and beer tent.

I strolled along the road where Miss P. lived in one of a pair of mellow cottages. Amazingly her sister was standing at the door and I attracted her attention. Phyllis would not come to the door to see me but she sent word that she would meet me at two o'clock. The cricket kept me occupied, but I could only think about her. When I saw her I was over the moon and we talked for two hours, but we still made no arrangement for the future. The time was not ripe. Later I heard that she had met a young man at the evening dance. Was I jealous!

One night on the train, by chance I met my old boss Mr. Peatman. He told me that he had just won a six month contract to provide bread for the barracks. Amazingly he wanted me to return to work for him and offered fifteen shillings a week living-in. Soon I paid a visit and accepted, thinking Miss Hard-to-Get would be nearer.

On the Saturday that I returned to Waddington, I found out that Phyllis had left with her parents for Scarborough. They were to help in her uncle's boarding house whilst someone was ill. So I had changed my job and still could not see her. However, I threw myself into the work anxious to show what I had learnt of my trade in the city. Certainly I had increased my skills in the confectionery and pastry side of the business.

At Peatmans we now baked bread an average of two hundred loaves a day for the Army, as well as those for our own village rounds. I was kept busy with the baking and only went on the rounds twice a week. Soon I was mixing with my old pals again and now felt top dog after two years of city life. Not for me the Sunday regulation gear of a navy suit, brown boots and cap!

Again arrogantly, I thought that I could take on any girl I liked. The local dances were the place to go. All the youths clustered at one end of the room and the girls at the other. I never could tell my right foot from my left and had no opportunity to learn. Eventually I managed to struggle through the waltz and fox trot but always felt awkward and embarrassed. I think I said "Sorry!" for treading on girls' feet more times that year than in the rest of my life. My hands always seemed to be so hot and sweaty too. I never mastered the Charleston or Black Bottom. Usually we only joined in when there was a Paul Jones, but had fun listening and reading rather bawdy verse and talking about sex and honeymoons. Even so I am sure our "knowledge" was far less than modern youth. We thought we were men-of-the-world. We drank ginger wine at threepence a glass.

After five months a friend told me they had seen Miss Phyllis Hard-to-Get on the bus. That meant she was staying with her cousin and so I promptly put a note through the letterbox, stating that I would be calling Saturday evening to take her to the Theatre in Lincoln. I never would take no for an answer and Phyllis was duly ready when I arrived. It was a Variety Show with some excellent turns. Miss P. said how nicely the violinist played and wished he had played for longer. I thought his semi-classical pieces were an unholy row but naturally I agreed with her. My taste in music had not yet gone beyond "Bye Bye Blackbird."

Phyllis, Edith and Sylvia about 1912 with parents, George and Susan Clarke and grandmother MaryAnn Tointon

Phyllis stayed for three weeks and we saw each other every night. We walked the lanes around Waddington, Harmston and Coleby (where she had been to school). Sometimes we talked but were often silent for long periods. Occasionally we smoked Craven A and would have a competition to see who could smoke a cigarette the quickest. There was no anti-smoking education then. It was very fashionable.

I had taken other girls around these same lanes but I dropped them all. They were not best pleased when I told them that Phyllis Hard-to-Get had beautiful hazel eyes and a figure like a pocket Venus. Yes, I was completely bowled over by her. She was less than three pounds when born but had survived - a remarkable feat at the beginning of this century. She grew to all of four feet eleven inches tall.

Three weeks later came the next shock. Miss P had obtained a post through an Agency to look after the elderly aunt of the Headmistress of a school in Hampshire. Another twist of fate for yours truly.

Chapter 18
"Chasing ... And Winning"

The Air Base at Waddington had been re-opened and many men contracted to the Air Ministry had descended on the village. Phyllis' war-widowed cousin, who lived with her father and nine year old son in a large thatched cottage there, had four of these contract men lodging with her. Three of them were married, but one "sly, undersized little rat" was single and was rather sweet on Phyllis when she stayed there. You can guess that my description of him may have been influenced by my jealousy. The home town of this five-foot two of skin and bone, "by coincidence" I was told, the very same Hampshire place where Miss Phyllis Hard-to-Get had her new post. So once more it was goodbye and gloom. Suspicions haunted me.

Netherthless, she wrote to me saying that she had arrived safely and was enjoying herself. She failed to state that she missed me. That weekend I tried without success to put her out of mind and went to the local hop. Every girl there snubbed me; no doubt justifiably, after the way in which I had made comparisons between them and Phyllis previously.

I was really fed up and the next day the Boss told me that, because he had been undercut, the Service Contract would not be re-newed. He would still keep me on if I accepted a lower wage. However, I scouted the Bakery Journal to find a job as near to Phyllis as possible since she was now two hundred miles away. The closest I could find find was one in Hertfordshire. I would only be seventy miles away across London. In those days in the Bakery trade it was usual for the advert to ask the applicant to "state wages required". I wrote offering my services as baker and roundsman - this time with genuine experience - at forty shillings a week. In a few days I received an offer of the job. I gave in my notice immediately and within a week I was preparing to leave Yellow-belly land for life elsewhere for the first time, not knowing that I would return later. It was an adventure for a lad who had not yet been outside his native county's borders, not uncommon then.

I do not remember any regrets about leaving my friends or the village but Miss Hard-to-Get was the spur. Changing trains in London was a great thrill and I arrived at my new workplace both excited and worried. This was a typical middle-class business community. The shop and restaurant was a rather imposing affair, painted in white and gold. I made myself known to my new employer, trying to seem confident but feeling very nervous. Nothing unusual in that, then or now.

He said, "I expect you're hungry so go and have a good meal in the restaurant." That seemed like a fair start. "When you've finished, and don't be too long, come in the bakery and we'll talk."

It was a large bakery with much more and modern machinery than Lincolnshire. When we had talked - or rather when I had listened - he said suddenly, "Is that your only suit your wearing?" When I replied that it was my best, worrying that he would not think it good enough he announced, "Well you'd better be careful not to mess it up. You can be packing those cakes into trays while we talk. "These bosses never miss a trick," I thought, hoping that one day I might become one. I was just nineteen.

After a five o'clock start the next morning, as part of a team of eight, I was put on moulding various shapes of bread. I thought I was as quick as the next man, but at six the Boss arrived and I was aware of him watching me. After a few minutes he said angrily: "You can go at the end of next week, You won't be any use to me."

You can imagine how I felt, being so far from home. The other men told me that the Boss was always in a bad mood at that time of morning and probably did not mean what he said. Anyway I spent more than two years working there and finally left of my own accord.

It was a very well-to-do area and some of the customers were quite different from those on my Lincolnshire village rounds. The "Big Houses" in my home county were far less grand than some I called on here. The lady of the house was hardly ever seen, since the tradesman was usually dealt with by the housekeeper and occasionally by the butler. On my rounds I had the custom of the Crosse and Blackwell family, one of the famous Foot households and the Smith Doreen's. Often they would have parties and order as many as forty long loaves at a time. I used to wonder what it would be like to have such a lifestyle, but knew realistically that I never would.

Miss Phyllis H.T.G was still uppermost in my mind and I wrote her a letter explaining where I had moved to. There came a quick reply which I opened with great anticipation. It simply said; "I hope you like your new job. I have enjoyed the good times we had together, but it's over now. Don't think too much of the past."

I was shocked and furious on the outside and of course blamed the "undersized rat" who was sweet on her, who hailed from the Aldershot/Farnborough area. Inside I was deeply upset.

In my reply, I told Miss Phyllis Hard-to-Get (and how true her nickname proved to be) that it was alright by me and I had finished crawling. Needless to say that is not what I wanted.

Soon, another letter arrived from Miss P. This time she announced that she wanted to continue writing and apologised, making the excuse that she must have been in a bad mood.

The saga moved on. A few weeks later I heard from her Lincoln cousin, Nancy, that P. had "left you for that hairy ape in town".

Was I jealous? No guesses needed.

We continued to write. I took comfort in the fact that all would be well since the ladies she lived with and went to Church and Social Club with, would be chaperoning her. This was no doubt extremely naive, but I had placed Miss P. on a pedestal and "knew" that I could trust her. I learnt that she had "a comfortable relationship" with the monster. For her eighteenth birthday I sent her a wristwatch which she "accepted only as a gift of friendship".

After a few months our letters became more and more frequent. Towards Christmas I suggested that I should visit her. She accepted, to my surprise, and she arranged for me to stay with some new friends of hers not far away.

In this wealthy area it was the custom for the Business customer to give generous Christmas boxes and I was lucky enough to receive them. An envelope marked "Baker" was left, usually on a tray, with the housekeeper for my Christmas call. I felt well-off compared to my early Lincolnshire days! I also got commission on flour sales and half a crown for every new customer. I like to think that it was my personal charm which persuaded them, but more likely they felt sorry for me.

Anyway I worked until very late on Christmas Eve, caught the train to Waterloo arriving at two o'clock in the morning. The waiting room was closed so I slept on a bench. The buffet opened at six so that helped. When I finally arrived, Miss P. was waiting for me, looking as pretty as ever.

Her friends made me extremely welcome and helped me overcome my shyness. It also helped that they had won in a raffle, a large hamper of Christmas Fare from Fortnum and Mason. Turkey, wines and spirits, Christmas Pudding and brandy butter and .... It was wonderful, but I could only contrast it with the food I had received as a child in Caistor Workhouse ten years before.

Miss Phyllis Hard-to-Get and I were left alone for a time in the lounge that evening. Whether the unaccustomed drink had given me courage or whether I had grown-up does not matter. After kissing her, I did the old-fashioned thing; went down on one knee and told her that I adored her and asked her to marry me.

Phyllis at last proved not so hard-to-get and accepted, but we decided not to become officially engaged until the following Easter.

Phyllis and Fred aged about 20

Chapter 18
"That Sinking Feeling... Is It All Over?"

We now wrote to each other every day. I used to send her "My Darling" cigarettes, violets or lily of the valley each week.

That Easter we met in London's West End, one of my few visits ever. Phyllis wore the ring I bought from a catalogue which she had seen. We bought a shilling guidebook. We thought it was very high class going into Lyons Corner House and were thrilled to bits. Phyllis chose lemon sole and chips with icecream and coffee to follow. I ordered the same and watched carefully what she did with the piece of lemon. At least she had been mixing with a few middle class people, I knew nothing of etiquette. The orchestra was playing "Carolina Moon" the hit of the moment. We always called it "our tune".

We enjoyed our day immensely and caused a laugh when we attempted to climb up the down escalator, but we were in love and happy.

Summer arrived. Phyllis had a fortnight's holiday and I managed to arrange my week to fit in with hers. We were going to spend part of my week at each of our our parents' homes.

My mother and Tom had moved into Market Rasen. They seemed to enjoy their new life: the shops, market day and various functions most days at the the large Chapels. My stepfather was the organ blower and received ten shillings every three months. This helped to pay for shoe repairs etc. They were still very hard-up. I wrote every month to tell them my news, which was usually exaggerated.

As usual in my trade, I had to work late on Bank Holiday Saturday. When I reached King's Cross the last train for Lincoln had left ten minutes earlier. So I had to leave the train at Grantham, twenty six miles away from the city.

I started walking, carrying a small suitcase and a brolly. By the time I had covered ten miles it was pouring with rain and pitch black. The umbrella was a help but I discovered that I had left a friend's borrowed camera on the train. In my pocket there was some rather squashed chocolate.

Soon the storm was over and I thought I glimpsed daylight. In those days in the countryside cars were still uncommon, particularly at night but eventually one overtook me and stopped to ask if I needed a lift. The driver turned out to be a Forces Officer from Farnborough, the same area as "skin and bone rat" and Phyllis lived in. We reached the City bus depot at six a.m. and the first bus to Rasen was at eight. The last sixteen miles seemed an eternity, but it was better than walking.

Phyllis was dressing and called down to me when I finally arrived. The telegram boy appeared with the wire, "Arriving Sunday Monday", which I had sent from King's Cross, about half an hour later.

We had a good time in those first few days. Another local Flower Show and Fete in a nearby village had the usual country games: greasy pole, tug-of-war and obstacle races. Two of the tallest men I have ever seen were being used to replace the pole on the High Jump. The band made us laugh as they were often out of tune. Some youngsters produced weird noises with their large brass instruments.

I told Phyllis about my first seaside visit to Mablethorpe on the parson's outing when I was at Newton Toft and my escapade under the pier. We decided to take a trip there on the bus. We spent the morning admiring the flower beds, riding on the various amusements and listening to the entertainers on the seafront. After lunch we pooled our remaining cash and took a boat trip on one of the local pleasure craft. These boats went out about five miles to a "Fort". We duly set off, twenty passengers and a dog. The boatman who must have been about seventy, assured us that, although the sea was choppy, it was quite safe. As we neared the "Fort", heavy clouds gathered. Thunder and lightning soon followed and the rain "siled" down.

The engine conked out and the heavy swell started coming over the side of the boat. The passengers on that side rushed over to our seats. Obviously this caused the vessel to list badly. The old "captain" tried over and over again to restart the engine but failed. He put the flag at half mast as a distress signal to the shore. Passengers began shouting to attract a distant trawler. Some grown men, as well as children, were crying. The dog and some people near me were sick and each time, I covered it with layer of tarpaulin. It was some sandwich. The waves got higher. I felt no fear and must have been young and stupid. Phyllis confided in me later that she was terrified and thought we would drown together.

Eventually the distress signal was spotted as we were long overdue. Another boat arrived alongside and the rescuer soon had the engine going again.

We were soaked by the sea and the rain and left very wet patches on the bus seats but arrived back in Rasen none the worse for our adventure. In the excitement both the gloves lent to me by Tom and Phyllis' umbrella had been left on the boat. We had a lovely day!

The next couple of days with Phyllis' parents were spent in the harvest fields. Her father George was a skilled, all-round farm worker and an excellent hedger. Although heading for seventy, he was still fully active on the farm. The home-reared boiled ham and the scalding hot tea from the large, blue enamel can tasted out of this world, so different from the powder in today's teabags. We read our fortunes from the tea leaves in the bottom of the cup. Of course, what we saw showed a bright future, even though we had no idea how to read the leaves and knew it to be nonsense anyway.

We enjoyed the long train journey back to London and said our fond farewells there. To save money, I had left my digs and had decided to take a room and fend for myself.

The months went by and we continued to to write to each other, but Miss Hard-to-get's replies seemed rather lukewarm. Then came a letter stating that the Headmistress she worked for had obtained a post in Derbyshire and that everyone would be moving there. I was upset, but comforted by the fact that she would not be seeing Pansy Face anymore. Several letters simply said that they had settled in but there was no invitation.

Out of the blue, a further letter arrived announcing it was all over between us and that she was returning the ring. I was stunned. I sent her a wire telling her that I would meet her in Nottingham the nearest town the following Sunday. By return telegram she agreed to meet me at the Bus Depot at three. So there was hope yet. I couldn't afford it but I stayed at The Gordon Arms. This event was important.

I was there at eleven hoping she would turn up early. I was obsessed. She duly arrived at three accompanied by her cousin Nancy. I suppose she needed moral support, but it certainly didn't help me. We walked and talked with Nancy a few paces behind like a chaperone. She insisted there was no one else and I believed her. Really she still could do no wrong in my eyes.

She was adamant. It was the end. I wanted to shake her but we parted and I arrived back in Hertfordshire at about midnight, sad and disillusioned.

Soon the customers found that a happy, smiling roundsman had turned into a sour uncooperative one. Such is love! I found that I was saving fifteen shillings a week and had money to spend on pleasures, but had no spirit for it. Sometimes I went to the pictures, a football or boxing match, or the local Rep. I rarely went in pubs as I disliked the taste of alcohol and smoky atmosphere. Occasionally, in a strange town for a match I would buy a sandwich and a glass of port. A man buying a glass of port for himself in those days, always got funny looks from the barman and other customers.

After a miserable three months, I decided to sell the ring. A Watford jeweller gave me three pounds for it. I remember travelling back on an open-topped bus with the rain pouring down. Total depression. The canvas cover over your knees soaked you worse than having no protection at all.

I felt this was it. Now I could get on with my life without any ties. Vowing that I would never be caught out again, I flirted with all the local girls and one in particular. Lily, who was Welsh, and I used to go out for walks and had good laughs together. Her mother always went to bed early so we would creep in. Lily would shout, "I'm home mum." Then we would put the gramophone on and have a kiss and cuddle. It was all very innocent in today's terms but we thought it was very risque. There was a lot of Heathcliff lurking in me. I felt the need to hurt somebody and often stood Lily up.

My twenty first birthday brought in the morning post, a present from my parents and bits and pieces from one or two girls. Then a surprise in the second post. A card arrived wishing me well from none other than Miss Hard-to-Get. This only served to increase the bitterness in my mind and I determined to let her stew.

Chapter 20
"Tramping and Dossing"

There followed a succession of jobs and I was generally run down. Second Pastrycook, door to door brush salesman, cold canvasser etc. etc.

Life was depressing until I swallowed my pride and wrote again to Phyllis. But Heathcliff still reigned as I enclosed a letter sent to me by Lily. It read "I long to be married, have a dream bungalow and a little boy with dark hair like his daddy."

You may guess that Phyllis returned that letter. She wrote she was "sure that Lily was the treasure of my heart". Years after she told me that she had gone around all day whispering to herself: "I won't forgive him."

Miss Hard-to-Get must have done because we were soon corresponding again regularly. In my next message I suggested that since we were now a pair again, I should come to Nottingham and find a job there. She agreed. I told her that I would take a walking holiday to meet her.

So it was, that I paid the rent and sent my clothes to my mother in Market Rasen and set off that Sunday morning. The evening before I had heard the airship R101 fly over and the next morning learnt of its fateful crash into a French hillside.

With only eightpence in my pocket, I bought a couple of rolls and some prawns which I was to eat that evening before sleeping under a haystack. It was very cold. Next day I walked on and the rain came down. That evening I dutifully attended the service in a roadside church. I cannot report that I was praying for my soul, my motive was free shelter out of the storm. That night's haystack sported a ladder so I was able to snuggle in. The following morning after a brush down and a wash in the stream, hunger overtook me. I plucked up courage to call at a house and ask for food and struck lucky. She produced two slices of bread and dripping which gave me the energy to take the next stage. I found an old tennis ball. Bouncing this, helped me to walk faster. In a way I was happy. London was being left behind and I was going home. I felt like Dick Whittington in reverse.

There followed a few more days of legging and sleeping rough. One morning on walking late because of fatigue, I was accosted by an irate farmer who had spotted me when ploughing. He threatened to have the law on me. That day I stumbled upon two tramps in a small spinney. They were making bacon and turnip stew. The inviting smell had led me to them and there was large red billycan of tea. Grudgingly they gave me a small mug of tea and told me that if I was hungry on the road, I should go in "Spike". Since I looked puzzled they explained that it was a place for vagrants near Melton Mowbray a few miles away. So I had walked through Bedfordshire and Huntingdon into Leicestershire.

Spike had no admittance until six o'clock but several down and outs had already gathered there like me. As soon as the attendant noticed me, he said that I looked so exhausted that he would bring me a mug of cocoa. I drank it greedily, Next, with three others, I was forced to have a bath in a large washroom. The attendant lectured me and advised me, as one so young , not to take up that mode of life. I was left with just my shirt on and more cocoa and bread provided.

I was led to a small, cell-like room. The door was locked and my clothes were left outside. The cell contained a very hard mattress with a large brown blanket for covering. The blanket smelt foul: sweat and stale urine. I noted the irony of being forced to have a bath and then sleep on a filthy mattress and blanket. However I was so tired that I slept until I heard the door being unlocked at seven the next morning. I collected my clothes, dressed and followed a number of others to the washroom. They looked like a cross-section of the human race at its worse. There was I in a double breasted, pinstripe suit. It was a bit crumpled, but seemed totally out of place among this group of the world's unfortunates.

After a bread and margarine breakfast, we were all set to work sawing and chopping wood. One chap refused to join in the work and paced backwards and forwards over a short distance. Someone explained that this was the length of the prison cell in which the character had spent many years. Bread and marg again for tea and that was the food for the day. We were locked in a large dormitory for the night. I noticed three huge pails in a corner. Next morning the buckets were full of urine and the stupid buggers kept using them even though they overflowed!

Yet more bread and marg for breakfast and a small packet of bread and cheese for our journey . Then we were allowed to leave.

These couple of days brought back vivid memories of my stay in Caistor Workhouse as a lad. I vowed to avoid such places in future, but when you're desperate.....

Chapter 21
"Phyllis Got!"

In spite of the doss-house conditions, I felt rested and refreshed. However I had walked many miles on "my holiday" and exhaustion soon set in. My left ankle was giving way and I was walking with limp. How scruffy I must have looked even in my suit.

To my delight a lorry pulled up later that morning. The driver said that he'd noticed me limping. "Would I like a lift into Nottingham?" So there was justice in the world. After some distance I noticed a signpost -- Nottingham seven miles. I'd walked over a hundred. He dropped me right in the centre in "Slab Square" and I thanked him for his kindness.

A letter was waiting for me from Miss Hard-to-Get in the Post Office. She would meet me at the bus depot on Sunday at two. This was Thursday.

Despite my scruffy appearance I found a hawker's job selling a clothes cleaning kit. The proposition was a packet of ammonia with a nail brush attached for a shilling. "Guaranteed to clean any suit or costume." My usual charm and sales talk - at least that's what I told myself - brought success with two customers.

I had enough for a shave at the barber's and I persuaded him to give me a haircut free since business was slack. This "wash and brush up" made me able to face the world. By Saturday evening I made a few bob. I had money and a job of sorts. A hostel provided a bed for the night for sixpence or a better room for a shilling. On Sunday morning I noticed men examining their shirts. One of them told me they were picking off the bugs. The men in this hostel were no less the products of an uncaring society than at the Spike.

Knowing I was meeting Phyllis that afternoon, I used the basement washing facilities for a strip wash for myself and for my shirt, pants, vest and socks. whilst I waited for them to dry on the heated cylinders, I managed to sponge down my suit. In the end I looked almost presentable. Some time before two that Sunday afternoon, Phyllis stepped off the bus. We kissed and I stared into those hazel eyes. I saw a look that I always believed would be there and I knew that Miss Phyllis had finally been "GOT".

We spent our afternoon talking and making plans as we strolled to the castle and along the river. I was determined to pay for tea and cakes in

Lyons. At the time I would rather have died than ask her to pay, but my pride suffered when we parted. I had no alternative but to give her my dosshouse address. We arranged to meet again the following Wednesday.

Only a few customers bought the "ammonia kit" on the Monday and Tuesday so on Wednesday morning I sold my watch for the princely sum of one and sixpence. Phyllis and I continued to meet on Sunday and Wednesday and for a long time she had no inkling of my parlous state.

In the meantime I went on the dole, but was told that I would receive only one payment of eight shillings and threepence unless I produced a birth certificate. At that time I thought my bastard origin still made me a social outcast and I hated having to apply to Sleaford District for a certificate which announced: "father unknown". But the Dole Office manager told me it was common enough. Things seem just as bad for the poor and needy under Thatcher's rule in the late eighties, as I write my story. Nothing really changes.

I was constantly hungry at this time and thought nothing of sitting opposite anyone whom I saw eating or cutting a loaf. If you stared at them long enough, they'd say, "Are you bloody hungry?" or something like that. You usually got a slice or two with marg or dripping. This was popular then and at most corner shops you could buy a quarter of beef or pork dripping. It was sliced from large flat trays and had a wonderful layer of jelly on the bottom. Nobody bothered about cholesterol then! But I still had to scrounge it.

To save money for my outings with Phyllis, I used to sleep rough some nights. At first I went with a group to sleep by the Trent but it was cold. Later I learnt about the brickyards out of the town centre. About ten of us slept in the kilns. The first night, I could not sleep because it was too hot! The burning sand made it impossible whichever side you slept on. I picked up a tip from the old hands. You placed a couple of bricks at one end and propped up a piece of zinc on them. This let a clearance of air through and I slept like a top after that. We had to be out by six in the morning and clear away the "equipment". The workers knew we came but never objected. They must have had sympathy with our predicament.

Later we walked back to the hostel and sneaked into the basement for a wash and brush down. If we could afford it, we bought a cup of tea there.

In time I discovered a convent a long walk away. If you rang the bell but did not speak to the person who answered the door, you were given a thick crust and mug of cocoa. I became one of their best customers. The walk was worth it.

Once a rather heavily-built cripple approached me at the hostel and announced that he knew of "quite a nice little lock-up job that could be broken into". I replied that I have never done anything against the law and did not intend to. One weekend I had no money at all and was desperate, since it was my Sunday tryst with Phyllis. I asked a cornet player if I could go busking with him. That morning we went to a very poor neighbourhood. He said that the poor always gave more than the rich. That's why the rich were rich. I wasn't with him long enough to know whether he was right. We spent the morning him playing and me collecting. He told me that if anyone asked why we were doing it, we should reply that we were both out of work because of the talkies - the cinemas not needing musicians anymore.

We took about four shillings each but when I gave the money he tapped my pockets to see if I'd kept any back. At least I got my share and could hold my head up with Phyllis that afternoon.

Finally my birth certificate came through and I got fifteen shillings a week. I had eight shillings to rent a room and seven for food. I couldn't afford to heat the place. Life was still hard and I wrote to Phyllis explaining that I was having to move back down south to sell Encyclopaedia on commission. She would have preferred me to be earning a regular wage but understood that beggars...........

It was Christmas before we saw each other again but we wrote often and there were no more petty jealousies. She was GOT. In between my book selling bouts down south, I now visited her at the School House at Ripley where she lived. Staying at my old digs in Nottingham I still had little money. Ever the gentleman I insisted on escorting her to and from Nottingham, on my two other necessary journeys. This meant two return trips for me so I developed a money saving dodge. I would get a twopenny ticket at the start of each appropriate journey and walk the remaining six miles. When I got back I would write her a letter, catch the last post and it would be on her breakfast table the next morning. Such devotion!

The offer of a baker and confectioner's job in Nottingham at three pounds a week sounded like bliss. Phyllis and I were over the moon but our joy was shortlived. At the end of the month I got my cards and was told the job was only temporary. Nevertheless we were used to such setbacks by now. She visited me at the digs on Sundays and it was there that we acquired our first piece of furniture. Phyllis saw an oak stool, almost big enough to be a coffee table. The landlord had made it for a relative who thought it too good for a kitchen stool. So we bought it for six shillings and still have it today.

Nearing twenty three, I suddenly felt the need to make a fresh start after all the problems of recent years. One day whilst walking in the park with Phyllis, it was decided. I would go home to Rasen and sign on there. Tom had given up being a chaff carrier and now had a job minding cows a mile outside town. Each smallholder who owned a cow or two had an arrangement that for the best part of the year, they were allowed to graze on the lane verges for a part of the day. Stepfather looked after sixteen of these cows and was paid a shilling a week per cow. Mother now spent a lot of her time with him for company. They seemed happy enough.

I duly signed on and received my fifteen shillings a week. Phyllis and I wrote to each other almost every day. Postage was three halfpence. During our erratic courtship we wrote about five hundred letters.

Phyllis also gave up her job and went back to live with her parents in Harmston. Ever the optimists, we decided that whatever happened we would be married the following Easter (1933). Each alternative weekend, I used to cycle the twenty six miles to Harmston to spend the weekend with her folks and she took the bus to Rasen to stay with mine on the following.

Then came a break. A small baker in town needed an extra man. It was a small firm employing one other baker and an errand boy. We mixed and baked the bread early morning, the other man delivered into the country in a motorised van and the errand boy went door to door with a hand truck in town. My job then was to make cakes and pastries during the rest of the day. This did me the world of good, because I had become very shaky in the techniques and it gave me opportunity to experiment with new ideas.

Now came the crunch that Autumn and Winter. I needed to save as much money as possible for the future. I'm afraid I did not pay mother as much for my board and lodging as I should have, but at least they ate better!

Savings grew but there always seemed to be something that stopped me from putting very much aside .. the story of my life and most other people's. I never smoked or drank.

At weekends when Phyllis and I met we used to pore over a Cash Furnishing Catalogue, and as the wedding day got closer, we would say, "Well we could do without a settee and a wardrobe". And so it went on.

I had started to "peg" a large black wool rug in the evenings. It was about seven feet long and fairly wide. The kit consisted of a large canvas backing and wool. You wound the thick black wool round a piece of wood about a foot long and then cut along the groove with a razor blade. All your wool was then the same length. I worked at this for week and eventually got so fed up that I used to give my mother twopence a row while I went to the pictures! Our wedding grew nearer and it was nowhere near finished so I decided to cut a foot and a half of the canvas. The rug looked out of proportion.

The milkwoman used to come round twice a day with a two wheeled truck. This carried two large churns of milk. Dipping a metal measure into the churn she ladled out your requirements into your own jug. I thought this milk was delicious but it probably wouldn't pass the regulations today.

It was a six weeks to our wedding. I asked the milkwoman if she knew of a house to let. She told me that a small shop in George Street was being converted into a private dwelling. We contacted the owner who told us it was promised but agreed that if that couple withdrew we could have it. "Go and have a look around," he said, and we arrived just as the workmen were scrubbing a red-bricked kitchen floor. The front room was small with a brand new wooden floor. We were delighted and just hoped. Was this fate?

Directly, we discovered that it was ours. On asking the rent we were told "six shillings and twopence a week." We were curious about the twopence and found that it was for the rates.

We paid for the rent for the next six weeks and were soon planning madly. We decided to stain the front room floor dark oak as we could not afford a carpet. After all we had my wonderful rug didn't we? The first free evening I started to stain the floor. I was so excited and rather naive. Having covered most of the floor, it dawned on me. The only exit was across my work. Treading warily to the door I had to cover up the footprints as best I could. Phyllis was too busy putting up curtains and generally fussing around as a new housewife to notice the problem.

The few items of furniture we could afford or had been given, arrived a week later. We had collected the wedding ring and the jeweller had given us some spoons. Phyllis had been measured for a dove grey costume. Being hard-up and practical, she had ruled out a white wedding.

The wedding was on Easter Saturday and the vicar decided he had to obtain the Bishop's consent. Since the vicar had caused us some apprehension, we did not invite him to the reception. It was 15th. April 1933.

On Good Friday I was exceptionally busy -- up at two a.m. baking hot cross buns until lunch time. Then I was baking extra bread and cakes for the holiday weekend. On the day of our wedding I was at work again at two in the morning and not able to relax until eight hours later.

I had hired a car to take mother, Tom and me to Harmston. Apparently Phyllis was having a nervous attack and refusing to dress until I arrived. My boss had kindly given us the wedding cake I had made. The other baker gave us a dolly peg and tub.

Our wedding was a quiet affair with only about twenty guests at the church and afterwards. We were married in Harmston Church where I used to wait for her when she was fourteen. Such a lot had happened since. Phyllis had a Matron of Honour and her young man acted as Best Man. We were presented at the Church door with the traditional wooden spoon

Fred and Phyllis's Wedding 1933

WEDDING AT HARMSTON.—The wedding took place at Harmston Parish Church on Saturday of Miss Phyllis Irene Clarke, the second daughter of Mr and Mrs G Clarke, of that village, and Mr Frederick William Marshall, the only son of Mrs J Lilley, of Market Rasen. The service was conducted by the Vicar, the Rev H Smith, and the bride was given away by her father. The duties of best man were discharged by Mr H Clarke, of Burgh, and Mrs Smithson, a cousin of the bride, was maid of honour. A reception was afterwards held at the home of the bride's parents, where a splendid wedding cake, the gift of the bridegroom's employer, Mr T H Ford, occupied the place of honour. There were a large number of presents and Mr and Mrs Marshall are making their new home in George Street.

Report in Market Rasen Mail

NOTE: The oak stool now serves as my telephone table and both the wooden spoon and dolly peg adorn my home..... *John Marshall*, son.

Chapter 22
"A Non-Bastard Appears"

The journey back to Market Rasen and our new George Street home was uneventful. We had a passenger -- a blue-grey kitten which Phyllis had adopted and called Peter. She used to say with some enthusiasm with visitors: "Of course I had Peter before I was married!" This raised a few eyebrows.

We arrived at about six. No honeymoon for us. Work and money did not permit but I did carry Phyllis and Peter across the threshold. We received numerous useful gifts from our parents mainly for the kitchen, a rolling pin and pastry board from Phyllis' older sister and a prize dinner and tea service delivered from Harrods from Phyllis' last employer, the Headmistress. This was completely out of our league.

We were up for Holy Communion the next morning and I was back at work on Easter Monday. There followed a year of bliss for me. After having been in digs since I was fourteen, to have your own little home with little wife to match the delight is hard to describe. I was becoming more responsible and we were gradually getting more ship-shape. We acquired an ironing board and her parents bought us some secondhand stair carpet. At Christmas I filled one of my Plus Four stockings with little presents and hung it on the bed head after she was asleep. This might be seen as sentimental but then I was and still am.

Life was contented and ordinary. We spent time with our neighbours on Sunday evenings. The man worked at the Corn Mill. His boss was our Landlord. We played cards for hours. We bought ourselves two racing cycles and most Sunday mornings cycled to the coast - Mablethorpe, Skegness and Cleethorpes. We cycled over to see Phyllis' parents in Harmston quite often too.

Her folks had moved to what were known as "Poor Houses". Five years before they had been almshouses provided by some benefactor but were now let at two shillings a week. There were about eight houses around a yard. Everyone shared two large outside toilets. They were a scream! They consisted of a large box for men, a medium for woman and a child size version but they were communal! They had a large recess below which had to be emptied from time to time. The smell was powerful. This was country life for the poor even in the thirties.

However, Harmston was a very attractive village. At the top of the hill near the Squire's Gates was a clear spring and close by was the village water pump. Most people used to take water from the spring for drinking purposes and years later when water was laid on in the streets with large metal pumps, many still used the spring. The end cottage of the "Poor Houses" had a system of water tubs arranged in decreasing sizes and each connected by a metal tube to the other. This ensured a plentiful supply of rainwater from the roof for washday and baths in front of the fire. There was no electricity. It was paraffin hanging lamps, free standing brass ones with globes and candles. The candle snuffers for extinguishing the flames they used were base metal and had handles like scissors.

Harmston was beautifully kept on the Squire's instructions. There were plenty of laurel and hydrangea hedges. There were ploughing matches and a local point to point nearby. A man would arrive from Lincoln with large bottles of ginger beer, dandelion and burdock and vinegar. He charged a shilling a bottle. Another sold paraffin and candles. The fishmonger came once a fortnight and the carrier's cart twice a week. Brown's Bus, an old London red bus, came on alternative days. If you wanted them to call, you hung a white rag out of the bedroom window. On a visit many years later, I noticed that the Hall, from which the Squire had ruled, had become a mental home and the old cottages had been demolished to make way for desirable residences for commuters. Later still, I learnt that the Mental Hospital had closed. Such is progress.

Phyllis' father George was now seventy (born in 1863) and about to retire. I made him a cake in the shape of a book and entitled it "Seventy Years by G.Clarke".

My employer decided to sell the business and I felt unsettled with the new owner's methods, nor did I take to his wife who looked down on the bakery part of the business.

I heard of a bakehouse that was to let. Phyllis and I spent hours   talking over over the idea of setting up a business ourselves. To us, it was a giant step but at last we decided to give it a try. We surrendered a small insurance policy and borrowed a little from my in-laws. I bought bread tins, trays and other essentials to make a start. Next I purchased a second-hand two-wheeled cart. It was a proud moment when I painted on the side; "MARSHALL'S HYGENIC BAKERY" in black and gold. We turned our front room into a little shop, as it once had been.

I fixed my cycle to the cart with a metal rod and loop under the saddle and set off that first day, with the cart loaded with bread and cakes. Canvassing a couple of villages, I found a good response. Disaster struck that afternoon when the cartwheels collapsed. I have never been very good on mechanics and that meant more expense. Phyllis tried to build up trade in the shop but it was still slow. I realised that the cart would be a problem in the winter, so I acquired a motorbike with a large box truck and separate sidecar. You simply had to remove four nuts and bolts to exchange the two alternating parts of the combination.

We had some good Sunday outings on it and, if I felt in the mood, I would really open her up. There was no speedometer! Once I turned a corner and the sidecar rose up off the ground and she was thrown out. She and the sidecar were so light that the outfit was unbalanced. There was some damage but amazingly she only suffered cuts and bruises. On another occasion I pulled into a garage for petrol and a motorist behind asked me if I always travelled on two wheels. "I've followed you for three miles and your sidecar has never touched the ground!" Happy times.

We began to realise that the business was making no real progress. I mentioned this to a commercial traveller who told me that he knew of a good job going in Sheffield. Phyllis and I could not hide our disappointment that our enterprise had failed. This was the first and last time that I was to have my own business.

The next Sunday evening we visited our neighbours. They had a large family of five children and the conversation came round to the possibility of our starting a family. After my beginnings, I boasted that we would never have a child and Phyllis agreed.

The next morning Phyllis walked across to the sink and vomited. Morning sickness had set in. She was pregnant. That settled it. We decided to cut our losses and finish. I accepted the Sheffield job.

We moved into a flat and began to enjoy City life. If we had a shilling left we took two seats in the "Gods" at the Empire or Lyceum - Max Miller, Ted Ray etc. We were still very hard-up, the story of our lives. It is very difficult to break out of the financial doldrums, but someone else's grief brought us luck. The boss knew a woman who lost twins at birth. We became the new owners of a pile of baby clothes and a pram with ball-bearing wheels. We were so proud.

Phyllis's time arrived and I rang for a taxi. It had just time to rush us to Nether Edge Hospital before taking a bride to church. We arrived at the hospital in a car bedecked in white ribbon. I think the staff must have wondered if the royalty was coming. For us it was!

John was duly born on 6th. August 1935. He was a "cot/kitchen baby" and very frail. He too had a shock when coming into this world. It was probably because he was the first known NON-BASTARD in my line, but THAT LITTLE BUGGER DIDN'T DIE EITHER!

Phyllis with son John 1935

What Happened Next?

Fred, Phyllis and John moved to Worksop, Nottinghamshire in 1939 where Fred took up a post as baker and confectioner at Goodliffe's opposite the Priory Gate and lived at 8 Abbey Street and later 75 Lincoln Street. John started school at Abbey Infants and Abby Boys. Phyllis worked at Batchelors' Pea Factory during the war. Fred's bakery job was a protected occupation so he did not serve in the armed forces although he was a prominent member of the ARP.

After the war, in 1946, the family moved to Stafford where Fred took up a post at the Bridge Cafe, next to the River Sowe. They lived initially in Ingestre Road, then at Holmcroft Road and finally Tixall Road. Fred later worked at the English Electric Factory and as an Insurance Agent. John attended St. Paul's Primary School and King Edward V1 Grammar School. In the 1960's both John and Fred became the first Liberal councillors for Littleworth Ward on Stafford Borough Council. John began his teaching career there and taught in Burton Manor, The Leasowes and Highfield Primary Schools.

In 1965 the family moved to Teignmouth in Devon when John took up a teaching post at Dawlish Junior School in Old Town Street. Fred and Phyllis lived in Headway Close and Fred was the manager of the Carlton Theatre Restaurant. Later he became a chef at the Royal Hotel. Granddaughter Polly was born to John and Glyn in 1974 and later became a teacher in Dawlish. Fred and Phyllis later moved to Old Town Street in Dawlish where they celebrated their Golden Wedding and spent the last years of their lives.

Postscript 1

Victoria dies in 1942 aged 55
Report from Market Rasen Mail

Link with the Jubilee.
  Friends and neighbours in Dear Street
joined with others who have known her
during her long stay in Market Rasen in
paying a last tribute to the memory of
Mrs Victoria Jubilee Lilley, the widow
of Mr Tom Lilley, whose death occurred at
the week end at the age of 54 years.
Mrs Lilley's unusual name commemorated
the fact that she was born in Victoria's
jubilee year. Before coming to the town,
Mrs Lilley lived at Toft. She was a
lifelong Methodist and had helped to
support many good causes. The funeral
was conducted at the Centenary Methodist Church by the Rev R N Smith and
the chief mourners were: Mr and Mrs
F Marshall, Worksop (son and daughter-
in-law), Mr and Mrs E Lilley, Harmston
(son and daughter-in-law), and Mr and
Mrs Clark, Harmston (father and mother).

Postscript 2

*Phyllis and Fred's Golden Wedding in 1983 in their Dawlish Home
(courtesy of Dawlish Gazette)*

Postscript 3

Phyllis, Edith, Sylvia. The last joint photograph, Selby 1993

Postscript 4

*John - Fred's son and
Polly - Fred's granddaughter
in 1995*